NONNA'S KITCHEN

NONNA'S KITCHEN

Annette Baccari

ADB Company - Annette Baccari
Annettebaccari@aol.com
FAX: 617-916-2764

COOKING MEASUREMENTS

Cooking Measurement Abbreviations

Abbreviations	Measurement
tsp	teaspoon
Tbsp	Tablespoon
fl	fluid
oz	ounce
pkg	package
c	cup
pt	pint
qt	quart
gal	gallon
lb	pound
sm	small
lg	large
sim	simmer

Cooking Measurements

Measurement	Equivalent
a dash	A teaspoon
a pinch	1/8 teaspoon
¼ stick butter	2 tablespoons
1 stick butter	½ cup
Juice of 1 lemon	3 tablespoons
Juice of 1 orange	½ cup

Cooking Measurement Equivalents

Measurement	Equivalents						
	Tsp	Tbsp	Fl oz	Cup	Pint	Quart	Gallon
tsp	1	1/3	1/6	1/48			
Tbsp	3	1	½	1/16	1/32		
oz	6	2	1	1/8	1/16		
cup	48	16	8	1	½	¼	1/16
pint	96	32	16	2	1	½	1/8
quart	192	64	32	4	2	1	¼
gallon	768	256	128	16	8	4	1

Contents

This cookbook is dedicated

To

My children: Gina, Ricky, and Filipp

And

To my late mother, Vincenzina Ruggiero Buono DiStasio, who was literally gifted in making a delicious gourmet meal out of nothing!

Thank you, Ma, for all that you taught us!

ANNETTE'S APPLE CAKE

Cook ahead:

4 apples (cored, sliced, or diced. Place apples in pan, than:

1 cup light brown sugar or white sugar	} Pour water on top of
1 level tsp cinnamon	) apples, sugar, butter,
1 Tbsp Butter	) and cinnamon. Stir,
¼ cup of water	} Cook for 2 minutes,
1 cup nuts (optional)	} covered, stirring a
	} couple of times

Add to the apple mixture above the cornstarch mixture (as follows):

   3 Tbsp of cold water

   1 full Tbsp cornstarch

Stir together until the cornstarch is completely dissolved into the water before adding to apple mixture. Add to apple mixture. Stir and cook for 1 more minute or until the water and starch mix have mixed in smoothly and is a bit on the thick side. (If you want to drizzle some of its syrup on top of the cake once it's cooked, add 2 Tbsp more water for extra juice.) Cool.

You can cook the apple mix a day or two ahead of time, so it's ready to use when you're ready to make the cake.

Cake batter:

Preheat oven to 350 degrees

Mix dry ingredients together in a bowl:

3 cups flour

½ tsp salt

1 tsp baking soda

1 tsp baking powder 1 cup nuts (optional)

Mix together well in large mixing bowl:

1 cup vegetable oil

2 tsp vanilla
½ cup apple juice (optional)
3 eggs
½ cup orange juice
1 cup sugar

Mix liquid portions well until blended. Add the flour mixture a little at a time until it's all mixed together well. You can either pour half of the batter into a Bundt pan, then half of the apple mix, the rest of the batter topped with the rest of the apple mix. Or you can mix the apple mix into the batter and bake.

Bake at 350 degrees for 1 hour or until cake springs back at the touch.

APPLE PIE

Preheat oven to 350 degrees.
This crust is always delicious and crumbly.

Crust:

2½ cups flour
¾ cup Crisco
Pinch of salt
¼ cup of cold ice water

Cut up Crisco into flour and salt mix until crumbly. Add the ice water and work in until it forms a ball, adding or sprinkling more flour or water if needed. Cut the ball in half. Place each half between two pieces of wax paper. With a rolling pin, roll out into the shape of the pie pan (round). Place in pie plate, pressing evenly against the bottom and sides of pie pan, and pinch the bottom with a fork. Bake for 5 minutes in a 350-degree preheated oven. Roll out the other half to be used as the top layer of the pie.

Filling:

7 apples (peeled, cored, and cut—I use a mix of Golden Delicious with any other apples that I have around)
1 tsp cinnamon
¼ tsp nutmeg (optional)
1 cup sugar
Butter

Mix sugar and cinnamon *and* nutmeg together. Place apples in the baked-pie-crust pan. Sprinkle the sugar mix all over, being plentiful, and dab a piece of butter on top here and there. Place the top pie crust layer and pinch onto the par-cooked crust. Make 3 or 4 slits on top, adding a toothpick to each slit to keep the slits open. Bake at 350 degrees for 45 to 60 minutes, or until the crust turns light brown and the juices start coming out of the slits.

BRANDY ALEXANDER PIE

Preheat oven to 350 degrees.

1½ cups chocolate wafer cookie crumbs
¼ cup butter or margarine (melted)
32 large or 3 cups miniature marshmallows
½ cup milk
1½ cups chilled whipping cream or Cool Whip
2 Tbsp dark crème de cacao or espresso coffee liqueur 1 Tbsp brandy

Mix crumbs and butter in a 9-inch pie plate; press firmly and evenly against bottom and side of pan. Bake for 10 minutes. Cool.

Melt marshmallows with milk over low heat, stirring constantly. Chill until thickened. In chilled bowl, beat cream until stiff, or use Cool Whip. Stir marshmallow mixture until blended. Gradually stir in crème de cacao and brandy into marshmallow mixture. Fold into whipped cream or cool whip. Pour into baked crust. Chill at least 4 hours before serving.

CUSTARD PIE

Preheat oven to 350 degrees.

2 cups milk (warmed)
5 eggs
¼ tsp cinnamon
¼ tsp salt
½ cup sugar Nutmeg
1 tsp vanilla

Make the pie crust (page 13). Place in a deep pie plate. Prick the bottom and sides with a fork. Bake for about 4 minutes. It will kind of bubble, but just lightly flatten it down with the back of a spoon while it's hot after you take it out of the oven.

Beat eggs slightly along with sugar until sugar is dissolved (don't overbeat—just whisk them). You could also add the sugar in the warm milk, instead of with the eggs, to let it dissolve. Add salt, vanilla, and milk, and blend well. Place the baked pie shell in middle rack of the oven. Slowly pour the mix into baked pie shell. Sprinkle nutmeg on top. Bake for 35 to 40 minutes or until toothpick inserted in center comes out clean.

PECAN PIE

Preheat oven to 450 degrees.

3 slightly beaten eggs
½ cup sugar
½ cup light brown sugar
½ to 1 cup light corn syrup (Karo) 1 tsp vanilla
¼ tsp salt
1 cup pecan halves
1 9-inch pie shell

Combine eggs, sugar, syrup (start with ½ cup), vanilla, and salt. Taste and add more syrup if needed for sweetness.

Sprinkle nuts in unbaked pie shell and pour filling over them.

Bake at 450 degrees for 8 minutes. Reduce heat and bake at 325 degrees for 30 to 40 minutes or until firm.

NANTUCKET CRANBERRY PIE

Lightly grease and flour a 10-inch-deep pie plate. Preheat oven to 350 degrees

In the bottom of plate, place:
2 cups cranberries (fresh or frozen) ½ cup chopped walnuts
½ cup sugar.

Mix:
2 eggs
¾ cup melted butter
1 cup sugar
1 cup flour
1 tsp vanilla

Stir until smooth. Pour egg mixture over the cranberries and walnuts.

Bake for 40 minutes at 350 degrees (a little longer if cranberries are frozen).

Delicious warm with ice cream.

ROCKY ROAD FUDGE BARS

Preheat oven to 350 degrees. Grease and flour a 13x9-inch pan.

Bar:

½ cup butter or margarine
1 square or envelope (1 oz.) unsweetened chocolate
1 cup sugar
1 cup Pillsbury's Best All-Purpose Flour*
½ to 1 cup chopped nuts
1 tsp baking powder
1 tsp vanilla
2 eggs

Filling:

6 oz. cream cheese, softened
½ cup sugar
2 Tbsp flour
¼ cup butter or margarine, softened
1 egg
½ tsp vanilla
¼ cup chopped nuts
6 oz. (1 cup) semisweet chocolate pieces, if desired

Frosting:

2 cups miniature marshmallows
¼ cup butter or margarine
2 square or envelop (1 oz.) unsweetened chocolate
2 oz. cream cheese
¼ cup milk
1 lb. (3 cups) powdered sugar
1 tsp vanilla

In a large saucepan, over low heat, melt ½ cup butter and 1 oz. chocolate. Add the remaining *bar* ingredients. Mix well. Spread into prepared pan.

In a small bowl, combine 6 oz. cream cheese with the next five filling ingredients. Blend until smooth and fluffy. Stir in nuts. Spread over chocolate mixture. Sprinkle with chocolate pieces. Bake 25 to 35 minutes or until toothpick inserted in center comes out clean. Sprinkle with marshmallows and bake 2 minutes longer.

In large pan over low heat,

Melt:
¼ cup butter
1 oz chocolate
2 oz. cream cheese
¼ cup milk

Stir in powdered sugar and vanilla until smooth. Immediately pour over marshmallows and swirl together. Makes about 3 dozen bars.

*If using Pillsbury's best self-rising flour, omit the baking powder.

ITALIAN CAKE

Preheat oven to 350 degrees.

3 eggs
1 cup sugar
1 stick butter
1 cup milk
2 cups flour
1 lemon, grated zest and juice
1 tsp vanilla
3 tsp baking powder

Cream the eggs, sugar, milk, and butter together. Add the remaining ingredients, and mix well by hand or with a wire whisk. Add lemon juice, zest, and vanilla. Mix well. Pour into a tube pan and bake for 45 to 60 minutes or until the center springs back. Dust with confectionery powder and serve. You may also cut this cake and fill it with your favorite filling or custard and sprinkling rum or brandy on each row/layer.

CRANBERRY PUMPKIN BREAD

Preheat oven to 350 degrees.
Grease (with Pam) and flour loaf pans.

1 cup canned or cooked pumpkin
1 cup sugar
¾ cup milk
2 eggs
1 tsp vanilla
¼ cup melted butter or margarine
2 cups flour
2 tsp baking powder
½ tsp baking soda
½ tsp ground nutmeg
½ tsp ground ginger (optional)
1 cup chopped walnuts (optional)
1 cup fresh or frozen cranberries (spread a mixture of sugar and flour over them)

In a mixing bowl, mix well the pumpkin, sugar, milk, eggs, and butter. Add vanilla and mix.

Combine dry ingredients and stir into pumpkin mixture. Fold in walnuts and cranberries. Pour into a greased and floured loaf pan.

Bake at 350 degrees for 60 minutes, or until toothpick inserted in center comes out clean.

Cool in pan for 10 minutes. Remove to a wire rack to cool completely.

PUMPKIN BREAD
Preheat oven to 350 degrees

Sift together and put aside:
3½ cups flour
2 tsp baking soda
1½ tsp salt
1 tsp cinnamon
1 tsp nutmeg
4 eggs
2/3 cup water
1 cup cooking oil (vegetable oil)
3 cups sugar
1 can pumpkin pie filling
Raisins
Nuts

Mix eggs, sugar, oil, water, and pie filling together with a fork or wooden spoon. Mix lightly. Add the dry ingredients and blend together. You may also add raisins and/or nuts to this recipe. Pour into two greased and floured loaf pans. Bake for 45 to 60 minutes, or until a toothpick inserted in center comes out clean.

PUMPKIN CHEESECAKE WITH BOURBON-SPIKED CREAM
Preheat oven to 350 degrees

Make the chocolate sauce ahead.

Chocolate Sauce:
½ to ¾ cup medium whipping cream (if you use the liqueur, use ½ cup)
1 Tbsp butter
½ pound semisweet chocolate chips
¼ tsp pure vanilla extract
1 tsp chocolate flavoring
1 Tbsp chocolate liqueur (optional)

Combine the cream and butter in a small heavy-bottomed saucepan over medium heat (I prefer using a double boiler—a smaller pan with the ingredients into a larger pan with 2 cups of water, that way you don't end up burning the chocolate). Heat the mixture until a thin paper-like skin appears on the top. Do not boil. Add the chocolate, vanilla flavorings, and liqueur. Stir until the chocolate melts and the mixture is smooth. Remove from the heat and let cool. Makes 1½ cups.

Crust:
1½ cups vanilla wafers or other flavored wafers or cookies you would like
  for taste, crushed into crumbs
1 cup ground pecan pieces
½ stick melted butter

Mix together with fork or by hand. Swish along sides of buttered springform pan, adding more to the bottom and pressing down with your hands.

Filling:
2 pounds (four 8 oz. packages) cream cheese, softened; or three 8 oz.
    packages Philly
1 lb. Ricotta or Farmers cheese
1 cup light brown sugar

½ cup of white sugar
6 eggs
½ cup medium cream
½ cup all-purpose flour
Pinch of salt
½ tsp cinnamon
1 tsp vanilla
2 cups pumpkin puree (1 can pumpkin pie)

In a mixing bowl, mix the cheese(s) until smooth. Add the sugars and blend well. Add the eggs one at a time. Add the cream and vanilla. Add the flour, salt, and cinnamon. Blend well. Add the pumpkin puree and blend well. Pour into prepared springform pan. Bake for 1 hour and 15 minutes or until the cake is set and toothpick comes out clean. Halfway through the baking time, loosen the sides from the pan to prevent the cake from splitting down the center. Completely cool before serving.

2 cups Cool Whip
Dash of bourbon or coffee liqueur or whatever flavor you like (optional)
1 cup semisweet chocolate sauce, warm (recipe above)

Combine the Cool Whip and liqueur together. Garnish cake with the bourbon, Cool Whip, and a drizzle of chocolate sauce.

RICOTTA PIE (Annette's)
(Makes one springform-pan pie or two regular-pie-dish pies.)
Preheat oven to 400 degrees.

Drain the ricotta for 2 days in refrigerator in a plastic drainer container before making this recipe.

Crust:
Crush enough Vanilla, almond wafers, or Amaretto cookies to use on bottom and sides of pan. Butter sides and bottom of springform pan. Sprinkle the crumbs on bottom and sides of pan. Swoosh the crumbs around so it coats the sides, adding more to the bottom and pressing down with the palm of your hand.

Ricotta Filling:
½ cup milk
2 lbs drained Ricotta
8 oz. cream cheese or farmers' cheese (optional)
1½ cups confectionary sugar
1 Tbsp flour
1 grated orange
1 grated lemon
2 tsp vanilla
4 eggs, separated

Beat egg whites with 2 Tbsp of confectionary sugar and ¾ tsp vanilla until foamy and thick.

Mix together well: milk, ricotta, cream cheese (and/or farmers' cheese), sugar, yolks, and flour. Add grated orange and lemon zests and vanilla to above. Fold the beaten egg whites into mixture. Pour into springform pan. Sprinkle leftover cookie crumbs on top (optional). Bake at 400 degrees for 20 minutes. Lower oven to 350 degrees for 45 minutes or until toothpick comes out clean.

I love to take a recipe and try different things with it. This is one of the recipes that I've done that to. I have been told that it's better than the store-bought Ricotta Pie from a pastry shop!

EASY CHEESECAKE
Easy and delicious!
Preheat oven at 350 degrees

1 package Duncan Hines Yellow Cake Mix or any brand name (do not use
   yellow *butter* cake mix)

Mix as directed on package and place in a greased baking dish/cake pan.

Ricotta filling:
2 lbs. Ricotta (drain in plastic drainer for 2 days)
4 eggs
1 cup sugar

Mix all together and pour on top of cake mixture. Bake for 45 to 60 minutes or until toothpick comes out clean.

This recipe was given to me by my oldest late sister, Vickie. My sister was a wonderful cook but didn't like to bake. However, when she did bake, you could be sure that it was going to be perfect and delicious! I couldn't believe how delicious and easy it was to make. I hope you enjoy it just as well.

BANANA CAKE (Annette's)
Preheat oven to 350 degrees

2 cups all-purpose flour
1 tsp baking soda
1 cup of white sugar
3 eggs
½ cup milk or sour cream
1 tsp baking powder
½ tsp salt
1 stick margarine or butter
¼ cup crème de banana liqueur (optional)
1 pkg. instant banana pudding
1 tsp vanilla
1 tsp banana flavoring
1 cup or 3 mashed ripe bananas mixed with
1 tsp banana and vanilla flavorings,
some white vinegar or lemon juice (1 Tbsp sprinkled all over to prevent it
   from browning),
2 Tbsp sugar
½ cup chopped walnuts or pecans (optional—I don't use this)

Sift together in a separate bowl: flour, baking soda, baking powder, banana pudding mix, and salt.

In a large bowl cream sugar and margarine well. Add eggs, flavorings, liqueur, and bananas with liqueur. Add to this ½ of the flour mix, then the sour cream or milk, and then the rest of the flour. Stir in nuts, if desired.

Spread batter into one greased cake pan or two loaf pans. Let stand for 20 minutes. Bake for 35 minutes or until top cracks along the top.

Drizzling:
Combine some confectionery sugar, banana flavoring, 1 tsp Crisco, and a little bit of cold water. Mix together, adding more water if needed for drizzling consistency. Crisscross on top of cake.

ZUCCHINI BREAD

Heat oven to 325 degrees. If your oven is slow, bake at 350 degrees. Grease and flour bread pans.

In a bowl, wash, dry, and shred/grate 2 zucchinis. Sprinkle some sugar over all and mix well. Set aside.

½ cup of pecan or walnuts (optional)

In a larger bowl, beat 3 eggs until foamy.

Add to the eggs and blend well:
1 cup of vegetable oil
2 cups sugar
1 Tbsp vanilla

Blend well.

In another bowl add:
3 cups flour (you can mix this flour with half white flour and half white wheat flour if you like—comes out equally delicious for any recipe)
½ level tsp cinnamon
1½ tsp baking powder
1 tsp baking soda
1 tsp salt
Raisins (optional)

Add the flour mixture to egg mixture. Add the grated zucchini and nuts. Blend well. Add raisins and blend well. Pour into greased and floured pan. Bake for 1 hour or until the middle comes out clean.

My late sister Vickie originally gave me this recipe that I have tweaked a bit with my own thoughts.

CHERRY CAKE SQUARES

Preheat oven to 350 degrees.
Grease bottom of pan.

3 cups flour
1 tsp vanilla
2 sticks margarine
1 tsp baking powder
2 cups sugar
4 eggs
1 can cherry pie filling

Cream together well the margarine and sugar. Add eggs one at a time and blend well. Add flour and baking powder and blend well. Add vanilla and blend well.

In a greased pan, pour ¾ of cake batter and spread evenly, then spread the cherry pie filling on top of the batter. Drop by spoonfuls the rest of the batter, spreading each of those spoonfuls a little but not completely covering the top. It has to have open spaces, with cherries showing here and there.

Bake for 45 minutes or until toothpick comes out dry and clean. Cut into your desired sizes. Delicious!

This recipe was given to me by my late in-laws closest friend, Nina. We would exchange recipes that were exceptionally good..

BLUEBERRY CAKE SQUARES

Preheat oven to 350 degrees.
Grease bottom of pan.

2 cups flour
1½ cups sugar
¾ cup of Crisco
pinch of salt
½ cup milk
2 eggs
1 tsp vanilla
2 tsp baking powder
1 can blueberry pie filling

Mix flour, sugar, shortening, baking powder, and salt. Add milk, eggs, and vanilla. Blend well. Pour ¾ of batter in greased pan evenly, then add blueberries. Dabble spoonfuls here and there with the rest of the batter over blueberries, but don't completely cover the top. It has to have open spaces, with blueberries showing here and there.

Bake for 45 minutes or until toothpicks comes out dry and clean. Cut into whatever sizes you wish.

TWEED SQUARES
Preheat oven to 350 degrees.

½ cup butter
2/3 cup sugar
11/3 cups flour
2 tsp baking powder
½ tsp salt
1 tsp vanilla
2 squares semisweet chocolate, grated
2 egg whites, beaten stiff
½ cup milk

Mix dry ingredients. Add milk and mix well. Add vanilla and mix well. Add chocolate then fold in egg whites. Pour into greased baking sheet. Bake at 350 degrees for 20 to 25 minutes and cool.

Icing:
1/3 cup butter
2 egg yolks
1½ cups confectionery sugar
1 tsp vanilla

Mix and pour over cooled cake.

Then in a pan, melt together:
2 Tbsp butter
2 squares of chocolate.

Pour over icing and refrigerate. Cut into squares and serve.

ANISETTE COOKIES
Grease and flour a 13x9-inch pan.
Preheat oven to 350 degrees.

Mix:
¼ cup milk
3 eggs
½ cup vegetable oil
1 tsp vanilla
2½ Tbsp anise flavoring
1 liqueur glass of anisette liqueur (optional)
2½ cups flour
1 cup sugar
½ tsp salt
1½ tsp baking powder
½ cup chopped nuts (optional)

Mix all together. Taste batter to see if you have enough anisette—
add more if you want a stronger anisette taste. Pour batter in pan.

Bake for 15 to 20 minutes. It will look whitish when done. Let it cool,
then pour frosting on top. You can sprinkle the top and then cut into
the sizes you want.

Frosting:
2 cups confectionary sugar
1 tsp Crisco shortening
3 Tbsp milk
1 to 2 Tbsp anisette flavoring
Mix until creamy and pour over cake.

*This recipe is easy and delicious. It will always make a hit. It was given to me
by one of my co-workers, Barbara, who had made it and brought it to my home
as an after-dinner dessert.*

CHOCOLATE CHIP COOKIES
Preheat oven to 375 degrees.

3 cups of all-purpose flour
1 tsp baking soda
1 tsp salt
1 stick margarine
½ cup of Crisco
¾ cup of light brown sugar
½ to ¾ cup of granulated sugar
1 tsp vanilla
2 large eggs
2 cups chocolate morsels
1 cup chopped nuts (optional)

Combine flour, baking soda, and salt in a bowl.

With wooden spoon or spatula, cream margarine and Crisco together until creamy, then add sugars and mix well. In a container, beat the eggs with the vanilla. Add to creamy mixture. Stir in flour mixture. Stir in chocolate morsels. Drop by rounded tablespoonfuls, or roll each in your floured hands and place onto ungreased baking sheet. Makes 36 to 48 cookies, depending on size.

Bake for 10 to 11 minutes or until light golden brown (they will not look cooked). Cool in baking sheet for 2 minutes longer. Remove to wire racks and finish cooling. Enjoy!

These cookies are sort of semisweet, so they really taste good!

CHOCOLATE CHIP CREAM CHEESE BARS

Preheat oven to 350 degrees.

2 frozen Pillsbury Chocolate Chip Cookie Rolls
2 8 oz. pkgs. Cream Cheese
3 eggs
1 Tbsp vanilla
7 oz. sugar (not quite a cup of sugar)

Filling:
Beat together the cream cheese, eggs, vanilla, and sugar. It's okay if the cream cheese doesn't all completely beat in well.

Cut the frozen chocolate chip cookie dough into ¼ or 1/3 inch pieces, and place them on the bottom of pan. Pour filling on top of cookie dough. Cut the rest of the cookie dough, and cover the top of the filling.

Bake for 35 minutes or until toothpick comes out clean. Cool. Cut into pieces and refrigerate.

My children, family, and friends love this creation! It's simple yet delicious.

FRUIT TART DESSERT
Preheat oven to 350 degrees.

1 cup flour
½ cup brown sugar
½ cup butter
½ cup pecan or walnut, ground fine
1 8 oz. package cream cheese
1½ cups confectionery sugar
2 packages Dream Whip
1 can pie filling (cherry, blueberry, pineapple—whatever choice you
    want, or all three)

Mix flour, brown sugar, butter, and nuts like a pie crust. Put in a 9x13
pan. DO NOT PRESS THIS TOO HARD.

Bake at 350 degrees for 8 minutes. Cool. Mix one large package of
cream cheese and powdered sugar. Then mix two packages of Dream
Whip with this mixture. Place this on top of sugar mixture. Put on top of
this one can of pie filling. Cut into pieces and place into paper cups
and serve!

*I came upon this dessert umpteen years ago when I was catering my children's
christenings and graduations, and I've been making it for all party celebrations.
They melt in your mouth and you can never get enough.*

COFFEE CINNAMON STRIPS

Make the dough one day ahead:
2 egg yolks
1 lb. butter (4 sticks)
4 cups flour
1 pint sour cream

Mix well and refrigerate for at least 4 hours or overnight. Preheat oven to 350 degrees.

1½ cups brown sugar
4 tsp cinnamon
1½ cups chopped walnuts or pecans (optional) or semisweet chocolate morsels
Raspberry and/or blueberry preserves

Sugar mix:
Mix sugar, cinnamon, and nuts together in a small bowl. Set aside.

Take out the dough from the refrigerator and divide it into four parts. Roll out each part of the dough onto a floured board or countertop and roll out into a circle. Cut each circle into eighths (cut circle in half, then cut each half into halves, and then cut each of those into halves). Spread some of the preserve from the widest end to the narrowest end, not quite reaching the end. Sprinkle the sugar/nut mix on top of the preserve. Roll from the widest end to the narrowest. Place each on a cookie sheet.

Bake for about 25 to 35 minutes or until lightly browned.

I know it sound like a lot to do, but it's so worth it! You won't regret it. I was given this recipe over thirty years ago and I'm still making it!

CONGO BARS (Squares)

Preheat oven to 350 degrees.

2¾ cups flour (or half white flour and half white wheat flour)
2½ tsp baking powder
½ tsp salt
2/3 cup shortening or butter (I prefer ½ cup)
1 box light brown sugar
3 eggs
1 tsp vanilla
1 cup nuts
1 pkg. semisweet chocolate morsels
1 cup dates, cut up (1 pkg.)
½ cup of raisins (optional)

Sift flour, baking powder, and salt.

Melt shortening and add brown sugar. Mix well and cool slightly. Add eggs, one at a time, beating after each addition. Add vanilla, dry ingredients, nuts, chocolate chips, and dates. Pour into a small sheet pan. Bake for 25 to 30 minutes. Cut in squares.

Makes 48 squares.

OATMEAL COOKIES
Preheat oven to 375 degrees.

1 stick of margarine
½ cup Crisco
1 cup light brown sugar
½ cup sugar
2 tsp cinnamon sugar
2 eggs
1 tsp vanilla
1¾ cups flour
1 tsp baking soda
1 tsp salt
2½ cups Old-Fashioned Quaker Oats
2 cups Rice Krispies cereal (optional)

OR

2½ cups Old-Fashioned Quaker Oats
2 cups nutty cereal (your choice)
½ cup raisins (optional)
½ cup nuts (optional)
½ cup semisweet chocolate morsels (optional)
½ cup of a nutty cereal (optional)

With a wooden spoon, cream margarine and Crisco, then add sugars and mix until smooth. Beat eggs and vanilla in a cup and add to sugar mix. Mix well. Add the flour, soda, and salt and mix well. Add oats (and Rice Krispies) and mix well. Add more oats if needed, for a bit stiffer dough but not dry. Roll one teaspoonful at a time into a ball in your hands or drop by teaspoonfuls onto an ungreased cookie sheet.

Bake for 10 to 12 minutes or until lightly browned.

CREAM PUFFS
Preheat oven to 400 degrees.

1 stick of butter
1 cup of flour
1 cup of water
4 eggs

Heat water and butter until it comes to a rolling boil. Do not stir. With a wooden spoon, stir in flour a little at a time until it forms a ball. Remove pan from heat. Add eggs one at a time, and mix well after each egg. You're supposed to do this with a wooden spoon, but I use a mixer. Drop spoonfuls onto cookie sheet and bake for 35 to 40 minutes. Cool.

Filling:
You can fill each puff with Cool Whip or with Italian cream below.

Italian cream:
Warm 2 cups milk in a pan (pan will be used as a double boiler).

4 eggs, separated (yolks in one pan, whites in bowl—to be beaten stiff
   with some of the flavorings and sugar)
1 cup sugar
6 Tbsp flour
1 tsp vanilla
1 tsp lemon (optional)
2 cups milk, heated

In one pan (this pan will go over the pan that you heat the milk in, so make sure it's a bit smaller so it fits over it), mix the egg yolks with a beater. Add the sugar, vanilla, and lemon flavorings. Mix well. Add the flour and mix well. This should be stiff. If it's not, add a little more flour until it becomes stiff. Add the warm milk a little at a time until you've mixed it all together. Scrap the sides to make sure you've gotten everything mixed in.

Add 2 cups of water to the pan that heated the milk. Put on high-heat surface. Place the pan that has the custard mixture on top of the pan with the water. The water will boil and cook the rest of the custard while you're stirring. Keep stirring until it becomes thick and smooth. Cool for an hour.

Stir a couple of times so the heat escapes.

Beat the egg whites with a beater. Add a little vanilla and lemon flavoring, along with some confectionary sugar, so it's on the sweet side when you taste it. Fold into the egg custard and combine well. Refrigerate. Use as needed to fill puffs or as a cake filling, or eat it by itself. Sprinkle some powdered sugar over puffs. Drizzle some chocolate syrup or your own chocolate-drizzle mixture over them if you like.

This sounds so hard to make, but it's a lot easier than you think. I always make a triple amount of cream because my family loves it so much by itself.

CARROT CAKE
Preheat oven to 325 degrees.
Grease and flour loaf pans, cake pans, or sheet pans.

Add in a bowl:
2 cups flour
2 tsp baking powder
2 tsp cinnamon
1 tsp salt

Add in another bowl:
1¼ cups vegetable oil
2 cups sugar
4 eggs
1 tsp vanilla extract

3 cups of grated carrots and 3 Tbsp sugar sprinkled into carrots

You can also add pineapple juice, crushed pineapple, chocolate chips, raisins, coconut, nuts, or whatever you like to this, but it's not necessary. It's just as delicious plain.

Mix bowls together. Add 3 cups grated carrots and whatever ingredients you want to add. Bake for 45 minutes-until center is done.

Cream Cheese Frosting:
1 stick margarine or Crisco
1 pkg. (8 oz.) cream cheese
1 box confectionary sugar or more, depending on how sweet you want the frosting to be.
2 tsp vanilla
1 cup chopped pecans or walnuts (optional)
2 Tbsp pineapple juice

Cream margarine, cream cheese, and sugar together. Add vanilla and nuts. Spread on cake, or leave out nuts and just sprinkle them on, or leave out altogether.

LEMON OR ANISETTE COOKIES, Annette's

Preheat oven to 400 degrees.

3 eggs
1½ cups sugar
3 tsp lemon or anise/anisette extract (depending on which you're making,
    add a little more)
¼ cup Strega, for lemon cookies
¼ cup Galliano, for extra taste in lemon cookies
¼ cup Anisette liqueur, extra for a stronger anisette taste in anisette cookies
5 tsp baking powder
4 to 5 cups flour
5 Tbsp vegetable oil
1 cup milk
1 tsp vanilla

Beat together eggs and oil. Add sugar, milk, and flavorings. Mix together flour and baking powder, and add this gradually to egg mixture till dough is firm but not sticky. Either roll bits of dough into walnut-sized balls or drop by spoonfuls on greased sheet. Bake for 10 minutes. I would cut this recipe in half. Taste dough to see if it needs more lemon, liqueurs, or anisette liqueur.

Frosting:

Mix to a frosting consistency: 4 cups confectionery sugar, 1 Tbsp Crisco, liqueur (Anisette for anisette cookies and Galliano or Strega for lemon cookies) and some cold water.

This recipe is my own creation for an absolutely delicious and lush lemon cookie.

CANNOLI

You need 4 to 6 cannoli sticks for this recipe.

Shells (can be made ahead and kept in fridge in a bag for 6 weeks):
3 cups flour
½ tsp cinnamon
1/3 tsp salt
2 eggs
2 Tbsp butter or oil
5 tsp sugar
1½ oz. sweet white wine (Riunite D'oro)
3 Tbsp water
1½ pints of oil for frying (mix vegetable oil with some olive oil)

On a wooden board or counter top, sift together flour, cinnamon, and salt. Make a well and add eggs, butter or oil, and mix well. Dissolve sugar in water, and add to flour mixture.

Knead on floured board or countertop until nice and soft and not sticky. Divide into two parts. Roll each part into very thin pie dough. Cut pieces that are about 2 x 2 inches and roll them around each cannoli stick. Drop into hot oil. It will bubble on one side, so you need to turn it to bubble on the other. Use a tong to hold the cannoli in place at the edges, so it doesn't come apart. Remove from oil and let it slide out onto paper towels by letting go of the tong slightly so you're not holding the cannoli so tight.

Cannoli filling:
2 lbs ricotta (drain for 2 days before adding to recipe)
Grated lemon
Bit of orange zest

Heat on medium heat:
1½ cups milk
¼ tsp cinnamon
a dash of nutmeg

a drop of almond extract
2 tsp vanilla
2 cups confectionary sugar
4 Tbsp cornstarch (blended in milk before heating)
Grated lemon and orange zests.

Mix together and heat until it thickens into almost a ball-like thickness. Remove and cool. When it's completely cooled (you can refrigerate this until you need it to finish making the filling), add 2 lbs ricotta and mix well.

You can cut this recipe in half. You can also add chocolate morsels and pistachio nuts on top of or into the filling. Sprinkle powdered sugar on top of cannoli and serve.

Remember that if you put the filling into the cannoli shells too early before serving, the shells will wilt and not be crunchy, so you want to fill them when you're ready to serve.

This recipe requires a lot of time to make the shells, or you can save yourself a lot of time and trouble by going out to buy the shells and filling them with your own filling.

CREAM CHEESE BROWNIES, Annette's

Preheat oven to 350 degrees.

2 8 oz. pkgs cream cheese
3 eggs
1 Tbsp vanilla
7 oz. sugar

Mix all together in a bowl and set aside.

In another bowl, mix:
1 pkg. brownie mix
½ cup water
½ cup oil
1 egg
½ cup Hershey's Chocolate Syrup 1 Tbsp instant coffee
½ cup of any cocoa you might have
1 tsp chocolate extract (if you have it)

Layer ¾ of the batter in pan. Add the cheese mix on top of this. Drop spoonfuls here and there with the rest of the brownie mix.

Bake for 30-35 minutes or until toothpick comes out clean. Cool.

FILLED COOKIES (Theresa's)

Preheat oven to 350° degrees.
You can cut this recipe in half.

½ cup sugar
8 Tbsp Crisco
4 eggs, beaten to a froth
4 cups flour
1 cup ice water
1 tsp baking soda
Pinch of salt

Sift dry ingredients into a bowl. Add Crisco and work in by hand or mixer. Add ice water, and work it through with fork until it's almost coming together. Add frothy beaten eggs that have been beaten with a little ice water, and mix with fork. DON'T OVERMIX! Roll out gently. Add your favorite filling preserve and roll up like a jelly roll. Brush with beaten egg/sugar.

Bake until lightly browned. Try 15 minutes first and keep checking every 5 to 10 minutes until it gets lightly browned. Cut each roll to a one-inch width, or thinner, pieces.

This recipe was given to me by my sister, Theresa. She is an excellent cook and baker in her own right and loves to cook, bake, and eat!

SOUR CREAM FILLED COOKIES (Nina's)
Filling (make ahead and refrigerate):

1 pkg. dates
1 medium jar strawberry preserves or jam

Place dates in a pan, and cover with enough water so it reaches the top of the dates. When water has absorbed, crush the dates well and add jam/ preserve. Mix well. This will be your filling. Set aside to cool.

Pastry dough:
Preheat oven to 350 degrees
5 cups flour
2 eggs
1 cup sugar
1 cup Crisco
1 cup sour cream
2 tsp baking powder
2 tsp baking soda
½ lemon, squeezed
1 tsp salt

Mix all together in a bowl or on a board. Knead gently until it forms a non-sticky ball adding a little more flour if need be. Break into 3 or 4 balls and knead each. Set aside. Roll each out about 12-14 inches long and 6-8 inches wide gently on floured board. The dough should roll easy for you. Spread filling all over and fold 3 times almost like a jelly roll. Place on ungreased baking sheet. Bake for 20-25 minutes or until lightly browned. Cool.

Frost with a mix of 2-3 cups of confectionary sugar, a tsp of Crisco, tsp of vanilla extract and enough cold water to make into a frosting consistency. Frost the whole baked cookie roll, adding colored sprinkle candies and then cut into pieces. Makes 12-15 pieces per roll. These cookies freeze well.

PIZZA DOLCE (Nonna Vincenza's Christmas Cheesecake)
Preheat oven to 350 degrees.

Crust:
1½ cups flour
2 eggs
1 Tbsp Crisco
½ cup sugar
2 liqueur glasses of Strega and Vermouth

Mix and roll out to a round or rectangle size to fit the pan you will be using. Place the crust into a Crisco-greased pan/dish. Dough should be a bit thicker for the bottom layer. Cut off hanging lengths. Save for strips for the top of the pie.

Filling:
2 lbs. ricotta (drained for 2 days)
2½ cups sugar
6 eggs
1 Tbsp vanilla
1 liqueur glass of Vermouth
1 liqueur glass of Strega

Mix all together with a fork. Taste. Make sure you can taste the liqueur. If it's just a faint taste, add more liqueurs. That goes for the sugar too.
Pour filling into pan/dish. Roll out the rest of the dough lengthwise into thin strips so you can make a lattice top.

Bake for 45 to 60 minutes. Cool and refrigerate.

No matter how much we try in our family, we cannot seem to come to the exact texture and taste that my mother's Christmas ricotta cake would come out to. God had given her a great gift for cooking and baking!

STRUFOLI (Christmas Bubbles)

Mix, on a floured board:
1 cup of flour
2 eggs
¼ cup olive oil
¼ cup sugar

Mix well. Cover and let it rest for 15 minutes or so on a floured board. Break off pieces, and roll them out into long pencil-length pieces. Cut this into 1-inch pieces.

Heat a deep medium-sized pan filled with ½ cup of olive oil and ½ cup Mazola Oil. Drop pieces a bunch at a time, not overfilling the pan. Keep turning them with a slotted spoon until they just start to turn golden blonde. Take them out, and place them on a paper-toweled dish. Drizzle with honey, add colorful sprinkles (optional) and confectionary sugar.

Keep in a cool spot until ready to serve, or serve as an appetizer.

ZEPPOLE (Christmas Dumplings)

Melt 1 tsp yeast in 1 cup of *warm* water with a little bit of oil and a ½ teaspoon sugar

Mix in a bowl:
2 cups flour
½ tsp of salt
2 eggs
1 tsp of yeast, melted in 1 cup of warm water with a little bit of oil
¼ cup of sugar

Fillings:
Anchovies— watered down to take most of the salt out
Raisins
Par-boiled sliced/diced apples
Dry cod pieces that have been in water for 2 or 3 days (changing the water
   daily)
Anything else that you would like to have in the middle of this dough

Mix all together well, cover and let it rise. I put it in the oven so there's no draft that will get to it. Keep it in the oven until it doubles/triples in size. It will be soft and bubbly. Drop whatever filling you want to put in the middle of each spoonful, and drop into a pan heated with olive/vegetable oil until lightly browned. Take out with a slotted spoon and place onto a paper-toweled dish. Sprinkle with sugar. I use a little bit of each of the above fillings.

FRIED RAVIOLI PASTRIES (Nonna Vincenza's—Christmas)

You can make these yearlong, but we traditionally make them for Christmas.

Filling:
2 lbs ricotta, drained for 2 days
2 egg yolks
1 cup of sugar

Mix all together and put aside.

Dough:
3 cups Flour
3 eggs
½ cup of sugar
¾ cups of ice water, more or less A bit of olive oil (2 Tbsp)
1 tsp Crisco

Mix all together and knead well. Break into 3 or 4 pieces. Roll out each into very thin layers. Drop the filling by teaspoonfuls across, leaving enough room at the top and in between to roll it over onto the filling and close them by fluting each with a fork. Cut them individually, and flute them on all open slit sides. Fry or bake in hot vegetable/olive oil mixture. Turn each as they start to color and fry on both sides, then take them out with a slotted spoon. Place them on a platter, and sprinkle sugar on top of each of them right after you place each on the platter. Cover and refrigerate. Let them cool before you eat them. Delicious

CRUSPOLE (Nonna Emilia's Bow-knot Crullers)

This recipe is a pain to make, but they are absolutely delicious and worth the work!

On a floured board or in a bowl, mix:
½ cup of white sweet wine (Riunite Gold or Bianco)
3-4 Cups flour (more or less, or you can use half white flour and half white wheat flour—delicious!)
3 to 6 eggs
¾ cup sugar
½ tsp salt
1/3 cup olive oil
1 liqueur glass anisette
2 tsp baking powder

Place a bottle of honey warming up in a pan of water—place whole bottle in water on low heat. The honey will loosen up for sprinkling.

Mix and knead all ingredients well on a clean floured board or countertop until smooth. Let it rest, covered, for at least 45 minutes or longer on floured board. Cut off small pieces of dough. Roll out to paper-thin on floured board, or in pasta machine on thin fine setting, into 8-inch strips and cut lengthwise. Make into a bow, and drop in heated deep pan of hot oil—vegetable oil with a bit of olive oil. They should bubble fast when you drop them in. Take and turn each on other side. These fry very fast, so be ready to take them out immediately or they'll overcook and get brown on you. Take them out with a tong or slotted spoon, and place them on paper-towel-lined dish. Sprinkle honey and powdered sugar over all when you have a good amount layered. Do this for each layer. When finished, wrap with Saran wrap all over, and store in cool or cold room/place.

SESAME OR POPPY SEED BREAD
Preheat oven to 325 degrees.

1 tsp vanilla
½ cup oil
3 eggs
½ cup sour cream
1½ cups sugar
Grated lemon peel

In a bowl, mix well oil and sugar for 10 minutes or until fluffy. Add vanilla, then add eggs, one at a time, beating after each, scraping bowl on and off.

Combine in a separate bowl:
1½ cups flour
¼ tsp baking powder
1/8 tsp baking soda
1 tsp grated lemon peel
2 Tbsp lemon juice
2 Tbsp poppy seeds or sesame seeds

Add flour mixture to batter alternately, with sour cream beating on low to medium speed until just combined. Pour into 2 greased or 1 large loaf pan(s). Bake for 60 to 75 minutes or until toothpick comes out clean. Cool and remove from pan.

CHOCOLATE CAKE SUPREME (Annette's)
Preheat oven to 350 degrees.

Mix all together in a bowl:
1 dark chocolate cake mix plus cake ingredients
1 instant chocolate pudding mix
1/3 cup chocolate or coffee liqueur
8 oz. sour cream
¼ cup cocoa
1 tsp chocolate flavor extract
1 tsp vanilla extract
1/3 cup Hershey's chocolate syrup
2 tsp instant coffee

Blend all together and mix at medium speed for 2 minutes.
Pour in greased Bundt pan. Cook for 30 to 35 minutes or until toothpick comes out clean.

Serve plain or with chocolate syrup swirled on top and Cool Whip or you may cut the cake in half or thirds and add frosting or vanilla or chocolate pudding for an unforgettable cake.

WACKY CHOCOLATE CAKE
Preheat oven to 350 degrees.

1½ cups flour
1/3 cup cocoa
1 Tbsp vinegar
1/3 cup vegetable oil
1 cup sugar
1 tsp baking soda
1 tsp salt
1 tsp vanilla
1 cup water

Sift dry ingredients into ungreased 9x12 pan. Make 3 holes in dry ingredients. Pour vinegar in first hole, vanilla in second hole, and oil in third hole. Pour water over all. Stir. Bake at 350 degrees until done (20 to 30 minutes).

Note: *In any given chocolate cake recipe, I like to add additional chocolates like cocoa, chocolate syrup, chocolate liqueur, etc. You don't have to, but it does come out even more chocolaty and tasty.*

COFFEE CAKE SUPREME (Annette's)

Preheat oven to 350 degrees.

In a bowl, mix together:

6 oz. semisweet chocolate morsels

2 Tbsp sugar

1 tsp cinnamon

In another bowl, mix:

2 cups flour

1 tsp baking powder

1 tsp baking soda

¼ tsp salt

In a mixing bowl, mix:

1 stick butter, softened to room temperature

3 eggs

1 cup sugar

1 tsp vanilla

Mix well.

Add half of flour and mix well. Add 1 cup sour cream and mix well. Add last half of flour and mix well.

Grease cake pans. Sprinkle some of the cinnamon/sugar/morsels on bottom of pan. Add ½ of batter. Sprinkle more of the sugar/morsels. Dab with pieces of butter or margarine on top of sugar mixture. Add remaining batter, and sprinkle the rest of sugar/morsels on top. Bake for 35 to 45 minutes or until cake is done.

This recipe has made it all the way to Windsor, Canada, and then some. I made it and brought it there when we went to visit my husband's side of the family. They loved it so that they requested the recipe, which they have shared with their family, friends, and their friends' friends.

CREAM CHEESE AND RASPBERRY COFFEE CAKE
Preheat oven to 350 degrees.

1 pkg. (8 oz.) cream cheese, softened
½ cup (1 stick) margarine or butter
1½ cups all-purpose flour
1 cup sugar
2 eggs
¼ cup milk
1 tsp baking powder
½ tsp baking soda
½tsp vanilla
½ cup seedless red raspberry preserves or strawberry preserves
Powdered Sugar

Beat the cream cheese and margarine together until completely combined. Add half of the flour to the cream cheese mix. Add the sugar, eggs, milk, baking powder, baking soda, and vanilla. Beat on low speed until combined, scraping the sides and bottom of the bowl on and off. Beat on medium speed for 2 minutes. Add in remaining flour on low speed just till combined. Spread batter evenly in a greased baking or Bundt pan. Dollop the preserves in small spoonfuls on top of the batter or, if you're using a Bundt pan, pour half of the batter in the pan, then the preserves, and then the rest of the batter. With a spatula or knife, gently swirl preserves into the batter to create a marbled effect. Bake at 350 degrees for 30 to 35 minutes or until toothpick inserted in center comes out clean.

LEMON DROP COOKIES (Angie's)
Heat oven to 325 degrees.

6 eggs
3 sticks of margarine
6½ cups flour
2 bottles lemon flavoring or anisette flavoring
1½ cups sugar
1 small can evaporated milk
5 tsp baking powder
1 lemon, grated and juiced
½ cup Galliano (optional)
½ cup Strega (optional)

Beat margarine, add sugar and eggs, and beat well. Add flavorings and lemon peel and mix well. Add flour (mixed with baking powder) and evaporated milk alternately, beginning and ending with flour, and beat well. Add more flour if need be. You want the dough to be on the soft side but not stiff and easily handled. Add liquors, if desired, and beat well. Drop spoonfuls onto ungreased cookie sheet. Bake for 10 to 15 minutes.

Frosting:
Mix well warm milk, enough confectionary sugar for all the cookies, lemon flavoring, drop of Galliano, and a ½ tsp of Crisco. It should be loose enough to drizzle on cookie or dip cookies in frosting on one side only. Sprinkle with jimmies. Yum!

Always taste the batter to make sure it tastes good.

The original recipe comes from my mother's best friend, Angie. I made some alterations. Angie had a bakery store in East Boston (no longer in business) and would sell these. At that time, they made the best bread, pastries, and pizza. She would use this recipe for the anisette cookies.

MACAROONS WITH PIGNOLI NUTS
Preheat oven to 350 degrees.

4 egg whites
½ cup sugar
1 cup confectionery sugar
1 lb. almond paste
1½ cups pine nuts

Mix all ingredients together, except for nuts, until smooth. Mix ½ cup of nuts in batter. Drop by spoonfuls or roll in your hands, wetting your fingertips on and off, or use a pastry bag with a large opening on ungreased cookie sheet. Make them as big or small as you like. Lightly press the rest of the nuts on each cookie.

Bake at 350 degrees for 15 to 18 minutes.

LEMON LOAF (Frances's)
Preheat oven to 350 degrees.
Grease and flour baking pans.

½ tsp Crisco or margarine
1 cup sugar
2 eggs
½ cup milk
1½ cups flour
1 tsp baking powder
½ tsp salt
1 grated lemon and juice
½ cup sugar

Cream: shortening, 1 cup sugar, and eggs. Beat well. Sift flour, baking powder, and salt until creamy. Add lemon zest and mix until smooth. Bake for 45 minutes.

Frosting: Mix ½ cup sugar with lemon juice. Pour by teaspoonfuls over hot cake. Invert cake and let it cool.

This recipe comes from a late friend of my sister-in-law's neighbor. She would make all these unusual and delicious baked goods that she learned as a young woman in Nova Scotia. I was fortunate enough to be the receiver of a few of her recipes.

JEWISH CAKE (Rowena's)

Preheat oven to 325 degrees. Bake at lower level of oven.

½ cup potato starch
½ cup cake meal
Juice of half small orange or lemon (grate the skin of half the rind of
  either)
1 cup sugar
½ cup confectionery sugar
8 eggs
2 Tbsp jam*

Separate the eggs, and beat the yellow until nice and light colored.
Add cup of sugar slowly until well beaten, then stir in the jam and
whichever juice you decide.

Beat the egg whites until stiff with ½ cup of confectionery sugar.

Stir the dry ingredients quickly into the yellows and stir well. Fold
egg whites in thoroughly. Be sure to get down to the bottom and fold
well because the mixture of the yellows and the meal is rather thick.

Pour into an ungreased and free-from-anything Bundt pan. Bake at
lowest level for 1 hour or until cake springs back to the touch. Do not
open before 50 minutes. Invert the pan onto a funnel or some
arrangement where cake hangs free. Leave until cool. Carefully use
spatula to free cake on all sides. Place on rack to cool a little longer.

*I used blueberry jam and orange, but I sometime use raspberry jam and lemon.

HARVEY WALBANGER COFFEE CAKE (Vickie's)

Preheat oven to 350 degrees.

1 yellow cake mix (not butter)
1 pkg. vanilla instant pudding (or regular)
4 eggs
¼ cup Galliano
¾ cup orange juice
¼ cup Vodka
½ cup vegetable oil
1 tsp vanilla

Mix all together well for 2 minutes. Grease pan, pour batter, and bake for 50 to 60 minutes or until well done.

Frosting: Confectionery sugar, warm milk or cold water, 1 tsp Crisco, and Galliano. Mix well and drizzle over cake.

WHITE FRUIT CAKE (Frances's)

This fruitcake tastes just like the Italian panettone. Delicious!
Needs to be made two months in advance of the holidays so the flavor
can seep in.
Preheat oven to 325 degrees.

1 lb. butter (creamed well)
2 cups sugar (added gradually to butter)
9 eggs (beat in one at a time)

Add flavorings:
3 Tbsp lemon
2 Tbsp vanilla
1 Tbsp almond

In a separate bowl, add:
3¾ cups flour
1 lb. pkg. blonde raisins
1 small pkg. mixed fruit
1 pkg. candied pineapple
1 bottle red cherries
1 bottle green cherries

Flour the fruit just before you put them in the cake, folding them in
by hand if need be. Cream butter with sugar and eggs. Add flavorings
and mix well. Add fruits and mix well. Pour into greased and floured
bread pans. Bake for 2 hours and 20 minutes. You can wrap them and
freeze them. They freeze very well.

If you enjoy panettone, you'll absolutely love this recipe. You have to make
this recipe no later than the end of October for December gifting or eating.
Not that you couldn't eat it earlier, but the longer you have it, the more the
flavor seeps in, just like a fruit cake. It's not heavy like a fruit cake but a lot
lighter and more flavorful.

M&M COOKIES
Preheat oven to 375 degrees.

1 stick margarine
½ cup Crisco
¾ cup light brown sugar
¾ cup white sugar
2 eggs
1 tsp vanilla
2½ cups flour
1 tsp baking soda
1 tsp salt
2 cups Rice Krispies
1 cup M&M's or semisweet chocolate morsels
½ cup chopped nuts (optional)

Cream margarine and Crisco well. Add sugars and cream well. Beat eggs and vanilla together, and add to creamed mixture. Beat until fluffy. Add flour that's been mixed with baking soda and salt. Mix well. Add Rice Krispies and mix well. Add M&M's and mix well. Drop by teaspoonfuls on ungreased baking sheet. Bake for 10 to 11 minutes.

BANANA LOAF (Frances's)
Preheat oven to 350 degrees.

½ tsp vanilla
1 tsp banana flavoring
½ cup Crisco or vegetable oil
1 cup sugar
2 eggs
2 cups flour
1 tsp baking soda
1 tsp baking powder
½ tsp salt

Mash banana with 4 or 5 drops of banana flavorings and distilled vinegar or lemon juice. Sprinkle some sugar and banana flavoring over them.

Cream Crisco or oil, sugar, and then eggs. Add vanilla. Mix flour, baking soda, powder, and salt. Mix into cream. Add bananas. Let stand for 20 minutes. Bake for 55 to 60 minutes.

NEW YORK CHEESECAKE (Annette's)

1½ cups all-purpose flour
1/3 cup white sugar
1 egg, beaten
½ cup butter, softened
2 pounds cream cheese, softened
1 pound ricotta or farmer's cheese
1¾ cups white sugar
3 tablespoons all-purpose flour
5 eggs
2 egg yolks
¼ cup medium whipping cream
Grated rind of ½ lemon

Directions:
Preheat oven to 400 degrees.

1. Lightly coat a 10-inch springform pan with spray oil.
2. To make the crust, combine 1½ cups flour, 1/3 cup sugar, 1 egg, and ½ stick of butter or margarine. Spread to the edges and bottom of pan. Prick all over with a fork, then bake for 10-15 minutes. Allow to cool.   Or:
3. Grease sides and bottom of pan with butter, then crush enough vanilla wafer crackers to cover sides and bottom.
4. Increase oven temperature to 475 degrees.
    In a large bowl, combine cream cheese, 1¾ cups sugar, 3 Tbsp flour, 5 eggs, yolks, and lemon rind. Mix thoroughly. Add cream and mix only enough to blend.
5. Pour filling over crust, and bake for 10 minutes at 475 degrees. Reduce temperature to 200 degrees and continue to bake for one hour. Turn oven off, and leave cake in for another hour. Don't worry if it looks a little jiggly in the center.
6. *Chill overnight*. This is imperative! If desired, top with your favorite fruit or serve plain when ready to serve.

WHITE OR CHOCOLATE FROSTING (Fluffy) (My favorite!)

1 cup sugar
1/3 cup water
¼ tsp cream of tartar
2 egg whites
1 tsp vanilla

In a small saucepan, combine sugar, water, and cream of tartar. Bring mixture to a boil over medium-high heat, stirring constantly till sugar dissolves.

In a medium mixing bowl, combine egg whites and vanilla. While beating the egg-white mixture with an electric mixer on high speed, very slowly add the sugar mixture. Beat until nice and thick or until stiff peaks form. Makes enough frosting to frost the sides and tops of two 8 or 9 inch cakes, or 1 Bundt-pan-size cake.

You can add cocoa or grated chocolate to make it into a chocolate frosting, or with chocolate and instant coffee for a mocha flavor!

BAKLAVA
Preheat oven to 350 degrees.

2 lbs pastry sheets (Phyllo sheets)

Filling:
2 lbs walnut meats, coarsely ground
1 cup sugar
½ lb. butter, melted

Combine nut meats, sugar, and rose water in bowl. Lightly butter bottom of large baking tray with butter. Place pastry sheets on bottom of pan, fitting it to edges. Lightly brush each sheet with butter. Repeat until you have used ½ of the pastry sheets, each one lightly brushed with butter. Spread nut mixture evenly over bed of pastry. Place remaining pastry sheets on top of nut mixture, again brushing each sheet lightly with butter. With sharp knife, cut in diamond shapes.

Bake at 350 degrees for 45 minutes to 1 hour or until golden brown. Brush with additional butter on top, and continue baking at 200 degrees for an additional hour and 15 minutes until top is light golden brown.

While pastry is baking, prepare syrup.

Syrup:
5 cups sugar
2½ cups water
½ lemon
1 Tbsp rosewater (you don't have to use this)

Boil sugar and water to make thin syrup. When almost done, add lemon half (and rosewater if you want). Cool before pouring over baklava. Pour over hot baklava. It will bubble all over. Serve when cooled.

CHEESECAKE WITH CARAMEL SAUCE, FLUFFY
(My favorite of the American Cheesecakes!)
I call it fluffy because it is not heavy, like a regular cheesecake, but nice and light so it melts in your mouth
Preheat oven to 325 degrees. Position rack to center of oven.

20 oz. cream cheese, room temperature
1¼ cups plus 2 Tbsp sugar
1 Tbsp grated orange peel
1 Tbsp grated lemon peel
2 tsp vanilla extract
4 large eggs, room temperature
5 large egg whites, room temperature

Butter 10-inch-diameter springform pan along sides and bottom. Crush as many of your favorite cookie wafers and swish around sides and bottom of pan, adding more on bottom and patting down with the palm of your hand. Wrap outside of pan with foil.

Using electric mixer, beat cream cheese(s) and sugar in large bowl until smooth. Mix in orange, lemon peel, and vanilla. At low speed, beat in whole eggs one at a time, stopping to scrape down sides of bowl frequently. Taste for sugar. Add more sugar if needed. Using clean and dry beaters, beat egg whites in another large bowl to soft peaks. Fold whites into cheese mixture in two additions.

Transfer batter to prepared pan. Set cake pan into large baking or cookie sheet pan. Pour enough hot water into the bottom of baking pan to come ½ inch up side of pan. Bake until cake is light brown on top and tester inserted in center comes out clean—about 1 hour 10 minutes. Transfer cake to rack and cool for 15 minutes. Using a small, sharp knife, cut around sides of pan to loosen cake. Release sides and cool cake completely. Cover and refrigerate cake overnight.

Caramel sauce:
1¼ cup sugar
1/3 cup water

1 cup whipping cream or medium cream
½ cup (1 stick) unsalted butter cut into small pieces, room temperature
1 tsp vanilla extract
¾ cup whipping cream or Cool Whip
2 Tbsp sugar (not needed if using Cool Whip)
3¼ oz. toffee candy bars, such as Skor, broken into pieces

Heat sugar and water in heavy medium saucepan over low heat, stirring until sugar dissolves. Increase heat and boil without stirring until mixture is a rich caramel color, occasionally swirling and washing down sides of pan with brush dipped into cold water—about 8 minutes. Reduce heat to very low. Add cream (mixture will bubble up) and stir until smooth. Mix in butter. Cool slightly. Mix in vanilla. Spread on cheesecake. Decorate with Cool Whip on the edges, leaving the caramel sauce showing in the middle. Delicious!

ROYAL PHILLY CHEESECAKE (Annette's—my second favorite!)
Preheat oven to 375 degrees.

Crust:
Graham cracker crumbs
1 Tbsp sugar
½ tsp cinnamon
2 Tbsp margarine or butter
¼ tsp nutmeg (optional)

Mix together and press firmly into a springform pan   *OR press*
your favorite cookie cracker crumbs—vanilla, chocolate, or almond
wafer crumbs.

Butter the bottom and sides of the pan and swoosh the crumbs all
over. Press the rest of the crumbs on the bottom of the springform
pan.

Filling:
1 lb. ricotta
2 8 oz. Philadelphia Cream Cheese
1 farmer's cheese
8 oz. sour cream
1 Tbsp vanilla
1 tsp lemon juice of half a lemon
1 tsp lemon zest, grated from 1 lemon
1 tsp orange zest, grated from 1 orange
2 ½ cups confectionery sugar
5 egg whites, beaten stiff with Confectionery-sugar
½ cup milk
1 tsp cornstarch
2 Tbsp flour
1 Tbsp sugar

Mix the 2 Tbsp flour, 1 Tbsp sugar, and 1 Tbsp cornstarch together
and set aside.

Cover the outside bottom of the springform pan that you will be using with aluminum foil.

Beat the cheeses, confectionery sugar, vanilla, lemon juice, lemon and orange zests, and sour cream together until well blended. Add the cornstarch, flour, sugar mix and blend well. Fold in the beaten egg whites with a wire whisk and pour into prepared springform pan. Place pan in a baking sheet or other larger round pan partially filled with water. Bake for 35 minutes at 375 degrees, then lower to 350 degrees and bake for another 30 minutes or until a toothpick inserted in center comes out clean. Shut the oven off, and let it stand in oven with oven door partially opened for 1 to 2 hours. Refrigerate. When you're ready to serve, add blueberry or cherry pie filling on top and serve! Yum!

DATENUT BREAD SUPREME
(My favorite of all datenut breads)
Preheat oven to 350 degrees.

2½ cups sifted all-purpose flour
1 tsp baking powder
1 tsp baking soda
1½ cups boiling water
1 egg
½ to 1 cup chopped walnuts
½ tsp salt
1 cup sugar
1 pkg. (1½ lb) pitted dates
3 Tbsp butter or margarine
1 tsp vanilla

Sift flour with baking powder, salt, and soda. Add sugar. Cut dates in fourths, pour boiling water over, add butter and let cool. Stir in dry ingredients, egg, vanilla, and nut meats. Mix lightly. Bake in a large greased loaf pan for 1 hour or bake in two small loaf tins about 35 minutes. Spread cream cheese when cooled.

CINNAMON STICKS (Annette's)

3½ cups of flour
½ cup white sugar
1 cup packed light brown sugar
1 Tbsp dry yeast
1 stick margarine, melted
1 cup milk
1/3 cup margarine plus 1 stick
½ tsp salt
Nuts (optional)
Raisins (optional)

Cinnamon/Sugar filling:
Mix 1 cup each of white and light brown sugar and 1 level tsp cinnamon together. (If you're going to add nuts or raisins to the middle of the pastry dough, take 1/3 of the mix out and save onto a large flat dish for rolling the outside of the dough in this.) Add nuts and/or raisins (optional).

Mix flour and dry yeast together in a separate bowl. Have 1 stick of margarine, melted, ready for brushing over each rectangle. Boil milk, ½ cup of white sugar, 1/3 cup margarine, and salt on medium-low heat until margarine melts. Once the margarine melts, remove from heat. Let it cool down to warm temperature. Add to flour mixture and mix well. Take dough out of bowl and knead on a clean floured board or surface, adding more flour until dough is easy to handle. Knead to a round ball. Grease the bowl you had the dough in with margarine. Place the ball of dough in bowl, turning it so it gets greased all over. Cover and let it rise for an hour or so. Knead again. Cut into 2 or 3 pieces. Thinly roll each piece out into rectangle shapes. Brush rolled-out dough with melted margarine or butter. Add cinnamon/sugar filling. Roll like a jelly roll. Melt one stick of margarine. Brush melted margarine all over. Roll completely into the cinnamon sugar. Cut into whatever size you want and twist each. Place on ungreased cookie sheet and bake for 15 to 20 minutes at 375° preheated oven. Remember that they will rise in size, so you want to roll them long and thin.

FRENCH TOAST, OVEN

This easy and delicious family favorite will warm the hearts of everyone who sits around your breakfast or brunch table.

5 large eggs, lightly beaten
¾ cup milk
1 teaspoon vanilla extract
1 tsp maple extract
2 tsp cinnamon/sugar mix
8-10 slices firm white bread, thick sliced

Topping:
¼ stick unsalted butter, softened; or ¼ cup of vegetable oil
1 cup light brown sugar, packed
3 tablespoons maple syrup or honey
1 cup pecans, coarsely chopped (optional)

Butter or spray a 9 x 13-inch ovenproof glass baking dish. Mix eggs, milk, vanilla, maple flavorings, and cinnamon/sugar. Dip bread slices in egg mixture. Place in baking dish. Pour any remaining egg mixture over bread. Refrigerate overnight. Preheat oven to 350 degrees. Mix butter/oil with sugar and syrup in a bowl. Stir in pecans. Spread topping over bread. Bake until golden, about 40 to 50 minutes. Let stand at least five minutes before serving. Serve with preserves, stewed fruit, or compote.

EASY MONKEY BREAD

Absolutely the most scrumptious concoction ever! Monkey Bread is well worth the mess every time. Kids love the gooey goodness! Adults gobble up the delicious hot buttery cinnamon sugar that melts in the mouth. This simple monkey bread recipe, made with refrigerator biscuits, will please all.

4 tubes (8 oz.) refrigerator biscuits (or two 16 oz. tubes like Grands)
¾ cup granulated sugar
¾ cup additional granulated sugar
1/3 cup brown sugar
¼ cup evaporated milk or milk
½ cup butter or margarine
1 teaspoon vanilla (optional)
1½ cups pecans or walnuts, chopped
2 teaspoons cinnamon

Preheat oven to 350 degrees. Grease, butter, or spray a Bundt, tube, or bread pan—preferably a pan with nonstick coating.

Mix ¾ cup white sugar and the cinnamon in a plastic bag. Cut biscuits into quarters (if using large biscuits like Grands cut into 6 to 8 pieces). Shake 6 to 8 biscuit pieces in the sugar cinnamon mix. Arrange pieces in the bottom of the prepared pan. Continue until all biscuits are coated and placed in pan. Do not pack pieces together, leave some space between the dough pieces for dough rising. If using pecans or walnuts, arrange them in and among the biscuit pieces as you go along.

In a saucepan, slowly bring milk, remaining ¾ cup white sugar, brown sugar, and butter/margarine and a little cinnamon to a boil, and cook for 1 minute. Remove from heat, stir in vanilla. Pour over biscuits in the pan. Bake at 350 degrees for 30 to 40 minutes or until golden brown on the top. Remove from oven and flip over onto a larger platter. Let sit with pan on top for a few minutes while the sweet mixture runs down the bread. Do not cut! The bread just pulls apart.

BISCUITS, BIG FAT JELLY
Preheat oven to 350 degrees

1 can Grands Buttermilk Biscuits
¾ stick butter or margarine, melted in a bowl
2 cups sugar
1 tablespoon cinnamon
1 container jelly, your favorite flavor

Spray a baking sheet with nonstick cooking spray. Combine the sugar and cinnamon in a zip-top bag and mix it up. Dip each biscuit first in the melted butter, and then drop into the bag of sugar one at a time and shake to coat. Place each biscuit on the prepared baking sheet and make an indention in the middle using the back of a spoon. Fill with your favorite preserves or jelly. Bake 13 to 17 minutes or until golden brown.

SNICKERDOODLES
Preheat oven to 350 degrees

3 tablespoons sugar
1 teaspoon ground cinnamon
1 stick margarine, room temperature
1½ cups sugar
2 large eggs
3 cups all-purpose flour
1 teaspoons cream of tartar
1 teaspoon baking soda
¼ teaspoon salt

Stir together 3 tablespoons sugar and cinnamon. Set aside.

Beat margarine and 1½ cups sugar at medium speed with an electric mixer until creamy. Add eggs, one at a time, beating just until blended after each addition. Combine flour and next three ingredients. Gradually add to margarine mixture, beating until blended. Shape dough into 1-inch balls; roll in cinnamon-sugar mixture. Place 2 inches apart on an aluminum foil-lined baking sheet.

Bake at 350 degrees for 8 to 10 minutes, or until lightly browned. Cool.

APPLE TURNOVERS Using Phyllo Dough

Preheat oven to 375 degrees.

4 medium apples, diced quite small (I use golden delicious)
2 Tbsp butter
2 tsp lemon/orange peel
1/3 cup sugar or more
1 tsp vanilla extract
1 Tbsp cornstarch
1 tsp cinnamon
½ pack of Phyllo sheets
½ stick of butter (more or less), melted
Powdered sugar for dusting

Peel, core, and dice apples.

In a medium saucepan, add apples, sugar, vanilla, orange/lemon peel, cinnamon, and cornstarch. Heat on medium-low stirring every so often. Cook for about 5 minutes or until the apple mixture thickens. Remove from heat.

Remove Phyllo dough from package and have a damp towel ready so you can keep the Phyllo sheets covered as you work. They tend to dry out very quickly. Melt butter. Using a pastry brush, brush one Phyllo sheet, the longer side facing you. Fold in half (vertical) and brush again. Fold again to form a long strip. Brush again with butter if you like. On one edge, add about 1¾Tbsp of apple filling. Roll in the form of a triangle, just like you would fold a flag. Brush the outside of the triangle Phyllo, and turnover with a little bit of butter. Place on a cookie sheet. Bake at 375 degrees for 15 minutes or until nicely golden brown. Check after 5 to 8 minutes so that they don't burn. Let cool and sprinkle with powdered sugar.

ALMOND BISCOTTI, Italian (Quaresimali)
Preheat oven to 375 degrees.

1/3 cup vegetable oil
¼ cup honey
2 cups granulated white sugar
2 eggs
¼ cup orange Juice
Zest from 1 orange, grated
2 tsp almond extract
3½ cups all-purpose flour, sifted
1½ tsp cinnamon
½ tsp cloves
1 tsp nutmeg
4 tsp baking powder
2 cups chopped or whole almonds
1 Tbsp milk

Bake almonds for 15 to 18 minutes on cookie sheet. Mix flour with baking powder.

Beat eggs with sugar, then add almond extract, orange juice and zest, milk, and oil. Mix well. Add cinnamon, cloves, and nutmeg. Mix well. Add flour mix and mix well with hands. Add almonds and mix well. Knead into logs and place on greased cookie sheet. Flatten each log a little. Brush each log with a mixture of egg whites, beaten with sugar. Bake for 10 to 15 minutes or until golden brown. Cool and cut into cookie size.

Delicious by themselves or with coffee.

NUT ROLL

Preheat oven to 350 degrees.
If you're a nut lover, you'll enjoy these!

3 lbs shelled walnuts
1½ cups granulated sugar
4 Tbsp honey
1 tsp vanilla
1 beaten egg
Pinch of salt

Grind walnuts and add the rest of the ingredients. Mix well. Place in pan and cover with milk so it covers the ingredients. Cook 15 to 20 minutes or until creamy.

Pastry dough:
4½ cups flour
1 tsp salt
2 egg yolks
1 cup butter
1 cup water
4½ Tbsp sugar
2 squares yeast

Mix and knead all together. Let it rest for 10 to 20 minutes. Knead again and let it rise for 1½ hours. Divide into 3 pieces. Roll out and spread filling. Roll up like a jelly roll. Place in pan. Brush with sugared egg white on top. Bake for 20 to 25 minutes.

ANNETTE'S IRISH SODA BREAD

Preheat oven to 375 degrees.

4 cups flour
1½ tsp salt
2 cups buttermilk
¾ cup of sugar
1 egg
1 cup raisins (that have been pre-boiled in some water to make them plumpy)

Mix together the flour, salt, sugar, egg, and buttermilk. Add raisins and anything else you might want to add. Mix well and knead until the dough is smooth and easily handled without being sticky. If the dough is sticky, add more flour and keep kneading until the dough becomes smooth and easy to handle.

Spray or butter bottom of pan. Add the dough. Spray or butter the top of the dough sprinkling a little bit of sugar or cinnamon/sugar mix (optional). Make a cross on the top of the dough and bake for 50 to 60 minutes, or until toothpick comes out clean when done.

ALMOND LEGEND CAKE
Legend has it that whoever gets the almond is assured of good luck.
Preheat oven to 350 degrees.

Cake:
½ cup chopped almonds
1 pkg. yellow cake mix (Pillsbury Plus)
½ cup orange juice
½ cup water
1/3 cup vegetable oil
½ tsp almond extract
3 eggs
1 whole almond

Grease pan. Press chopped almonds on side and bottom of pan.
In a large bowl, combine cake mix, juice, water, oil, extract, and eggs.
Mix at low speed. Beat 2 minutes at high speed. Stir in the whole
almond. Pour batter into pan and bake for 35 to 45 minutes.

Glaze:
½ cup apricot preserves
2-3 tsp orange juice
½ cup chopped almonds (optional)
½ cup confectionary sugar

Combine all ingredients and beat well. Pour over warm cake. Cool
completely and serve.

WHEAT PIE (Easter)

Soak ½ lb. of shelled wheat grain for 3 days changing water each day and then cook for 1 hour or until it gets tender—found in Italian stores or nature food stores
Preheat oven to 350 degrees.

Crust:
3 eggs
2 cups flour
4 Tbsp Crisco
½ cup sugar
3 tsp baking powder

Mix all together and knead. Roll out to measure your pan size. Grease pan sides and bottom with Crisco. Roll out 3/4 of the dough so it will cover the bottom and sides of your pan. Roll out the rest of the dough and cut into lengths that will fit your widths and lengths for crisscrossing for lettuce top.

Filling:
Cooled cooked wheat
2 lbs. ricotta
7 eggs
2 Tbsp vanilla
1 grated orange peel zest
1 grated lemon peel zest

Mix all together. Taste for sweetness—it should be on the sweet side. Pour into pie crust pan. Add crisscross pieces of dough spreading them 1 to 2 inches apart.

Bake for 45 to 60 minutes or until center toothpick test comes out clean.

DOUGHNUTS

Preheat 1 cup of vegetable oil mixed with a little olive oil in a deep frying pan.

½ cup milk
½ cup Bisquick
1 egg
Vegetable oil

Mix all ingredients together. Drop the batter in by teaspoonfuls. Take out when lightly browned. Pat off the oil. Roll in confectionary sugar.

PRETZELS
Preheat oven to 425 degrees.

Mix together:
1 tsp dry yeast or 1 pkg
1½ cups warm water
1 tsp Sea Salt
1 Tbsp sugar
4 cups flour

Put yeast in a cup. Add warm water and sugar. Mix with a fork and let it bubble up. In a large container, add flour and salt and mix. Add water with yeast and mix well. Knead on floured board. Cut into sections, rolling each and making whatever pretzel shape you want with them.

Brush tops with beaten egg. Add coarse salt or sea salt on each. Bake for 12 minutes.

PEPPERMINT WAFER COOKIES (Greek)

(This recipe can be cut in half) Different and delicious!
Preheat oven to 325 degrees.

3¼ cups flour
1 tsp baking soda
½ tsp salt
½cup (1 stick) butter
½ cup Crisco
1 cup sugar
½ cup light brown sugar, firmly packed
2 eggs
2 Tbsp water
1 tsp vanilla
48 chocolate Andes Mint wafers

Sift flour, soda, salt. Cream butter with shortening. Add sugars, then unbeaten eggs, water, and vanilla. Blend in sifted ingredients. Mix well and chill for at least 2 hours or overnight. Enclose each mint wafer with 1 Tbsp of dough. Place on ungreased cookie sheet 2 inches apart. Top with a walnut and bake for 10 to 12 minutes.

GREEK COOKIES
Preheat oven to 375 degrees.

1 lb. unsalted butter or margarine
3 Tbsp Crisco
1¼ cups sugar
4 tsp baking powder
2 egg yolks
1 jigger scotch
½ cup orange juice
1 orange grated zest from 1 orange
½ cup water
1 tsp cinnamon
1 tsp vanilla
4 to 5 cups flour
1½ cups chopped nuts

Cream butter/margarine, Crisco, sugar, and yolks. Melt cinnamon in water. Add water in blender and add orange juice, scotch, orange zest, and mix together. Pour into bowl. Add flour and nuts. Mix well. Make balls the size of walnuts. Bake for 12 minutes in ungreased cookie sheet. Roll in powdered sugar while hot. Before serving, roll again in powdered sugar.

BRAIDED PASTRY (Annette's)
Preheat oven to 350 degrees.

4 cups flour
1 cup sugar
¼ cup olive oil
¼ cup milk or buttermilk
 4 tsp baking powder
¼ cup rum, brandy, or anisette (your choice)
1 Tbsp vanilla
6 eggs
1 cup sour cream
Raisins (optional)
Nuts (optional)
Filling of your choice

Mix flour and baking powder together. Place on wooden board or clean counter top. Make a well and add the rest of the ingredients. Mix and knead well. Let it rest, covered, for 20 to 30 minutes.

Cut in 3 pieces. Re-cut each piece into another 3 pieces. If you want each pastry to be small/ medium, cut those again. Roll each out long and a little wide. Place filling (cinnamon-sugar mix, with or without raisins, and with or without nuts, preserves, whatever you like) in center of each and close and roll each up.

Take 3 filled lengths and braid them together. Brush tops with 2 eggs beaten with 2 Tbsp sugar or honey. Bake for 20 to 30 minutes. Frost with beaten confectionary sugar, milk, ½ tsp Crisco, 1 tsp vanilla, or leave plain.

PEANUT BUTTER COOKIES

Preheat oven to 375 degrees.

¾ cup Jiff Creamy Peanut Butter
½ cup Crisco shortening
1½ cups packed light brown sugar
3 Tbsp milk
1 Tbsp vanilla
1 large egg
1¾ cups all-purpose flour (Pillsbury Best)
½ tsp baking soda
¾ tsp salt

Combine peanut butter, Crisco, brown sugar, milk, and vanilla in bowl. Beat at medium speed until well blended. Add egg and blend well. Combine flour, baking soda, and salt. Add to mix at low speed. Drop by rounded teaspoonfuls, 2 inches apart, onto greased baking sheet. Flatten slightly with fork, making a star pattern with the edge of the fork while flattening.

Bake 7 to 8 minutes or until just beginning to brown. Cool 2 minutes and serve. Makes 3 dozen.

PEANUT BUTTER BALLS
One can never make enough of these little creatures!

1 stick of melted butter or margarine
1 pkg. confectionery sugar
2 cups peanut butter
3 cups Rice Krispies

Mix all together well. Form into balls, whatever size you want.

Chocolate Coating:
1 bag semisweet chocolate morsels (12 oz.)
1 small block paraffin wax

Melt chocolate and paraffin wax together in a double boiler. Keep the heat under simmer for the melted chocolate. Layer a piece of wax paper onto a cookie sheet or counter. Dip the balls individually into the chocolate with a slotted spoon, and place each on wax paper. Cool. Serve. Keep refrigerated.

TWISTS
Preheat oven to 350 degrees.

Cut 1 cake of compressed yeast into 3 cups of sifted and measured bread flour and ½ lb. unsalted butter at room temperature.

Stir in 3 egg yolks and 1 cup light coffee cream.

Mix thoroughly with a wooden spoon. It is not too sticky to handle with the hands. Divide into six balls and wrap individually in wax paper overnight or for up to three to five days.

Mix thoroughly together:
1 cup sugar
2 tsp Cinnamon
1 cup of finely Chopped filberts (hazelnuts) or walnuts or pecans

Bring the dough to room temperature. The nut mixture gives you about two cups worth. You have 6 pieces of dough, so take 1/3 cup of the nut mixture and place it on a piece of wax paper, adding more nut mixture as it diminishes. Roll one piece of dough at a time lightly onto the nut mixture so the nut mixture covers the whole ball. Place that ball between two pieces of wax paper, and roll it out round like a pie crust but on the thin side. Cut into eight, and roll like a crescent roll, from the wide end to the narrowest end. You can make minis and cut each into 16 pieces instead of 8. Place on a greased cookie sheet, and bake at 350 degrees for 20 to 25 minutes.

DANISH PUFF PASTRY
Preheat oven to 350 degrees.

1 cup sifted Gold Medal flour
½ cup butter (1 stick)—for flour
2 Tbsp ice water
½ cup butter (1 stick)—for melting with water
1 cup water
1 tsp almond flavoring
1 cup sifted Gold Medal flour
3 eggs

Measure first cup of flour into bowl. Cut in butter. Sprinkle with 2 Tbsp water and mix with fork. Round into a ball, and divide in half. Pat dough with hands into two long strips, 12 × 3. Strips should be 3 inches apart on ungreased baking sheet.

Mix the second amount of butter and water. Bring to a rolling boil. Add almond flavoring, and remove from heat. Stir in flour immediately to keep it from lumping. When smooth and thick, add one egg at a time, beating until smooth. Divide in half, and spread one half evenly over each piece of pastry on baking sheet. Bake about 60 minutes, or until topping is crisp and nicely browned. Frost with a confectioner's sugar icing, and sprinkle generously with chopped nuts.

Venture out and try spreading a filling in-between the two sheets of pastry.

SEVEN-LAYER BARS
Preheat oven to 350 degrees.

Place:
1 stick butter or margarine in baking sheet and melt in oven.

Sprinkle over the butter or margarine:
1 cup graham cracker crumbs
1 cup coconut
1 pkg. (6 oz.) chocolate bits
1 pkg. (6 oz.) butterscotch bits

Drizzle on the above:
1 can condensed milk
1 cup chopped nuts (optional)
1 cup miniature marshmallows

Bake for 30 to 35 minutes. Cool before cutting.

BLUEBERRY COBBLER
Preheat oven to 375 degrees.

Filling:
¼ stick of butter or margarine
1 Tbsp lemon juice
5 cups blueberries
¾ cup sugar

Place butter or margarine in an 8 × 8 square glass baking dish and melt in microwave or oven. In a bowl, mix lemon juice and blueberries. Add sugar, and mix well. Add blueberry mixture to baking dish over melted butter or margarine. DO NOT STIR.

Topping:
1 cup flour
1 cup sugar
1 tsp vanilla
½ cup milk

Combine all of the topping ingredients in a small bowl. Pour this mixture over the blueberries, and bake for 45 minutes or until brown. Serve with whipped topping or vanilla ice cream.

PECAN OR WALNUT BREAD LOAF
Preheat oven to 350 degrees.

1 Stick of margarine
¼ cup Crisco or ½ cup vegetable oil
1 cup sugar
2 tsp baking powder
1 tsp salt
3 cups flour
1½ cups pecans or walnuts, broken up
2 eggs, beaten with vanilla
1 tsp vanilla
1½ cups milk

Mix flour, baking powder, and salt together. Cream shortening and sugar together for 1 minute. Add beaten egg with vanilla, and mix well until it all comes together. Add half of the flour mix and mix well. Add the milk and mix well. Add the rest of the flour mix, and mix well. Add nuts and mix well. Pour into greased and floured loaf pans.

Bake for 45 to 60 minutes.

NON BAKING DESSERTS

SUMMER ANGEL FOOD CAKE

1 angel food cake or pound cake (I prefer angel food)
1 16 oz. can of Del Monte fruit cocktail
2 pkg. vanilla pudding (I prefer My-T-Fine, if you can find it. I prefer to
   cook my pudding, but you can use the instant too.)
1 pkg. of cherry Jell-O or dark cherry Jell-O
1 strawberry Jell-O or 1 raspberry Jell-O
Large Cool Whip container

Three days before you're going to serve this cake, make the Jell-O, combining the two flavors together. Refrigerate, covered, and let it partially jell so when you test it, it sticks on your finger.

Cut the angel food cake in ½ -inch slices. Layer them in a lasagna aluminum foil pan. Drizzle the juice from the fruit cocktail all over the cake just to slightly cover the cake pieces but not enough to make it wet. Add the Jell-O and spread it all over the cake. Add the fruit cocktail, and then the vanilla pudding, and refrigerate. On the day that you'll be serving the cake, add the Cool Whip on top, refrigerate, and cut in pieces when you're ready to serve it.

STRAWBERRY-BLUEBERRY ANGEL FOOD CAKE

1 angel food cake
2 quarts of strawberries, washed, sliced in threes
1 pint of blueberries
1 envelope of Sweet'N Low or Equal
Karo corn syrup
Large Cool Whip container

One day before you're going to make this cake, wash and cut the strawberries into a bowl. Add the washed blueberries, eliminating any of them that are not good or are moldy. Sprinkle the low-sugar envelope over them. Drizzle some corn syrup over all and mix. Taste for sweetness, and then cover and refrigerate.

When you're ready to assemble the cake, cut the angel food cake in slices and arrange them in a lasagna pan. Drizzle some of the juice from the berries over the cake slices. Add some berries all over, then the Cool Whip, and repeat the layer, ending with a few berries on top of the Cool Whip. Cover and refrigerate until ready to serve.

I usually make this two days ahead of time so the flavor can seep in and makes it much tastier.

BLACK AND WHITE ANISETTE COOKIES DESSERT

2 pkg. of soft anisette cookies

2 pkg. vanilla pudding (I prefer My-T-Fine—if you can find it), cook
   it and cool

2 pkg. dark chocolate pudding (I prefer My-T-Fine—if you can find
   it), cook it and cool

Brandy (I prefer Stock Brandy)

Three days before serving this cake, slice the anisette cookies in half, keeping the same shape of the cookie. Layer them in a deep dish or lasagna aluminum pan. Drizzle some brandy (I use stock brandy) all over, then add the vanilla pudding. Repeat the layer of cookies, drizzling the brandy over them, and then adding the chocolate pudding and ending with spreading the Cool Whip on top of the chocolate pudding. Keep refrigerated until you're ready to serve.

You can shave some chocolate pieces on top of the Cool Whip, but it would be only for looks. The cake is absolutely delicious in itself.

ANGINETTI DELIGHTS DESSERT

1 pkg. of Stella D'Oro Anginetti cookies
4 oz. cream cheese
4 oz. Cool Whip
8 oz. can of crushed pineapple

Mix the cream cheese, Cool Whip, and pineapple together (reserving the juice from the pineapple). Drizzle some of the pineapple juice on each cookie. Fill the center with the whipped mixture, and serve! You can also drizzle some brandy or rum on the cookie before adding the filling to make it even more interesting.

SORBETTA (Italian Sherbet)

This is not your ordinary sherbet. This is made only in the wintertime with clean snow.

To make the sherbet or *sorbetta*, you need to have the syrup made ahead of time and ready for use.

Syrup for red sherbet:
A bottle of homemade or bought red table wine 2 cups of sugar or more.

Boil wine and sugar until sugar is melted. Taste for sweetness. It has to be really sweet, so if it tastes just a little sweet, add another cup of sugar. Cool. Pour in jars, cover tightly, and store in a cool place until you're ready to use it. I usually make this in the Fall.

When the snow comes, take off the top thin layer of snow and scoop up a big bowl of snow, being careful not to go to the bottom of the layer of fallen snow (you only want the middle part of the snowfall.) Add enough syrup to cover the snow, mix and serve.

Syrup for lemon sherbet:
1 quart of water
4 lemons (grate the skin, and then squeeze each lemon and add to water) 2 to 3 cups of sugar

Boil the water, lemon zest, lemon juice, and sugar until sugar is melted and tastes very sweet. Cool. Pour in jars, cover tightly, and store in a cool place until you're ready to use it.

When the snow comes, take off the top thin layer of snow and scoop up a big bowl of snow, being careful not to go to the bottom of the layer of fallen snow (you only want the middle part of the snowfall.) Add enough syrup to cover the snow, mix and serve. Or you can make some crushed ice and add the syrup to that, freeze, then crush it up for an Italian Slush.

LEMON LUSH DESSERT CAKE

1 pkg. lemon cake, any brand name
2 pkg. lemon pudding
1 lemon, grated skin zest and juice Cool Whip

Bake your cake according to directions, except add half of the lemon zest and juice to the cake mix in whatever size baking pan you want (Bundt, round, rectangular, etc.). Bake and cool. When it's completely cooled, cut the cake in half so you can fill it with the lemon pudding.

While the cake is baking, make your lemon pudding, adding the rest of the lemon zest and juice. Cool completely. Add to the bottom layer of the lemon cake. Add the top layer of the cake onto the lemon pudding. Refrigerate until ready to serve. Before serving, top with Cool Whip, cut and serve.

MEAT, PASTA, SALAD, FINGER FOOD, AND PUNCH RECIPES

Some Italian tongue twisters from my father:

Apelle figliolo d'Apollo
fece una palla di pelle di pollo
tutti i pesci venniero a galla
per vedere la palla di pelle di pollo
fatta d'Apelle figliolo d'Apollo

Nell' A.D. 333
trentatre trentini andavano
su per trento tutti e
trentatre trattando
Ripeto:
Nell' A.D. 333
trentatre trentini andavano
su per trento tutti e
trentatre trattando

Modestino DiStasio

CHICKEN CUTLETS, ANNETTE'S—You're Gonna love these!

Freeze boneless chicken breasts slightly for easy handling. Cut each breast to whatever thickness you like.

Cut your cutlets one or two days ahead of time, and keep them refrigerated in a bowl covered with cold water until you're ready to batter them but not for longer than 2 days.

In a frying pan, heat 1 cup of Mazola corn oil with ¾ cup of Filippo Berio olive oil (not extra virgin) on medium high heat.

Add to first bowl (for 12 cutlets):
3-4 cups of *fresh* Italian grated breadcrumbs—or more
1 Tbsp parsley
Salt and pepper to taste
¼ to ½ cup of Grated Romano and Parmesan cheeses

Mix all together and taste for salt.

Add to second bowl:
5 Eggs
Salt and pepper to taste
2 Tbsp very fine cornmeal flour
2 Tbsp each of Romano and Parmesan cheeses

Mix all together until eggs have been well beaten.

Dip each cutlet into egg batter, and then into bread crumb mixture. Place on platter. Preheat oil on medium-high heat. Fry two to four at a time, depending on the size of your frying pan. Fry each side for 1 to 2 minutes each, turning each side twice or until it's slightly golden colored. Place on paper towel as they're cooked. Serve hot or cold. Delicious! Perfect plain or for chicken parm.

THANKSGIVING TURKEY

Preheat oven to 350 degrees.

Rinse and soak whole turkey for an hour in salted water. I use a clean sink and leave it with a wet cloth soaked from the salted water to cover the turkey. Cut wings off and use for soup.

Flour the bottom of the turkey pan. Add, over the flour, 2 sliced onions, 1 diced clove of garlic, salt and pepper and 2 cups of water. Stir. Grease turkey all over with a piece of bacon, pork fat (or butter, which I don't use), or Crisco. Place turkey on top of the onion mixture. Stuff the turkey with stuffing that follows below, and sew it with thick white thread and thick needle.

Place slices of bacon on top of turkey and wings. Cover with aluminum foil. Bake for 1½ hours, than start basting the turkey with its own juices. Baste every so often, leaving aluminum foil crinkled just on top of turkey <u>after</u> the first 1½ hours. Add more water if it needs it. Bake at 20 minutes per pound or until tester pops.

Filling (mix in a bowl):
3 cups fresh Italian breadcrumbs 1 finely diced clove of garlic
½ to 1 cup raisins (optional)
½ cup grated Parmigiano (Parmesan) cheese
½ cup grated Romano cheese 1 tsp parsley
Salt and pepper to taste 2 Tbsp of olive oil
5 eggs
You may also add ricotta to this recipe (2 Tbsp) if you wish.

Mix all together well. Taste for salt. If it's too wet, add some more breadcrumbs. Stuff turkey. Sew turkey end with an extra large needle so stuffing doesn't come out as it cooks. Or use your own favorite stuffing.

STUFFED CABBAGE

Boil a whole head of savoy cabbage in a deep pan with 3 cups of salted water, covered, for 15 minutes. Cool.

Mix in a deep bowl:
1 lb. of 85 percent ground beef
3 sweet Italian sausage meat, squeezed out of its casing
¾ cup of boiled jasmine rice (boil in salted water w/a bit of oil, and cool)
1 to 2 eggs for moisture
1 clove of garlic, finely diced
1 onion, finely diced
Salt and pepper for taste
¼ cup of grated cheese and extra for sprinkling over cabbage rolls
1 Tbsp parsley
A little olive oil, maybe 2 Tbsp
2 sweet Italian sausages, each cut into 4 pieces
4 cloves of garlic

Mix beef, sausage meat, rice, eggs, garlic, onion, salt, pepper, parsley, ¼ cup of grated cheese, and olive oil together well. Put aside.

Pull apart the head of cabbage, leaf by leaf. I cut the thick middle end part of the leaf off for easier rolling. Place 1 or 2 tablespoonfuls of the mix in each leaf. Roll, placing the cabbage sides to the middle as you roll, and place in pan. Do the same until you finish the mix or the cabbage leaves. Sprinkle grated cheese over all. Crush the 4 garlic pieces and throw here and there on top of cabbage rolls. Throw the 2 cut sausages over top of cabbage rolls. Lay 3 to 4 slices of bacon on top of this. Lightly sprinkle some oil over all. Cover with aluminum foil. Bake at 350 degrees in a preheated oven for 45 minutes. Remove foil and bake for another 45 to 60 minutes or until cabbage rolls are a little golden brown.

Always delicious!

ZUCCHINI AND POTATOES

Sauce:
4 Tbsp fresh or dry mint
1 onion, diced
1 clove of garlic, diced
Black pepper
Red pepper flakes (optional)
1/3 cup of olive oil
1 cup of kitchen-ready tomatoes (Pastene) or fresh tomatoes
salt to taste

Take 2 to 3 zucchinis, cut in half lengthwise, and then cut, in thick pieces and salted, 4 to 5 golden potatoes, cut in half, and then quartered, and salted.

Make your sauce: Fry the onion and garlic until it starts to wilt. Sprinkle a little black pepper and/or red pepper flakes. Add the mint and cook for 1 minute. Add the tomatoes. Add salt to taste. If the tomatoes taste acidy, add a ½ tsp of sugar. Add the quartered/salted potatoes. Cook for 5 to 8 minutes. Add the salted cut zucchini. Mix, cover, and cook until potatoes and zucchini are cooked. Serve by itself or with bread.

PASTA AND BROCCOLI RABE

Pasta: Penne, rotini, shells or whatever type of pasta that you like

Trim the bottoms of rabe; wash and cut up the rabe into 1 to 2 inch pieces. Set aside. Boil the pasta in boiling water adding salt and a drizzle of olive oil. Cook for 8 minutes or until al dente. Drain and set aside.

Sauce:
1 to 2 cloves of garlic, diced
½ cup of virgin olive oil or regular olive oil
½ cup of chicken broth
Red pepper flakes, as much as you like or none
Salt to taste
Grated Parmesan cheese

Fry the garlic until lightly colored in olive oil. Remove garlic from pan. Add chicken broth, red pepper flakes, salt, and rabe pieces. Cook for 5 minutes, stirring on and off in a partially covered pan. When the rabe is tender, pour over pasta, sprinkle with Parmesan cheese and serve. Make sure you taste the rabe for salt before pouring over the pasta.

MINESTA AND CORN BREAD

1 large pot
4 2-inch pieces of pepperoni
Pork spareribs (as much as you want) or pork pieces <u>with bones,</u>
preboiled in
  salted water until tender
Grated cheese
Corn bread (page 147)
Head of Savoy cabbage
½ cup olive oil
4 to 6 crushed pieces of garlic
Sweet and/or hot sausages (optional)

Wash the outer leaves of the cabbage, cut in half, and then in half again. Quarter the rest of the cabbage, cutting out the center of the cabbage core.

In a deep pan, fry the garlic in olive oil until it starts to turn color. Add the pepperoni and 1 cup of warm water. Add some salt to taste. Let it cook for about 20 minutes. Add cabbage, spareribs and salt, about 1 tablespoon or to taste, and cover, stirring on and off so everything is combined. If you have any pieces of hard cheese left over that you don't know what to do with, add it into the pot. Cook until cabbage is tender.

Once the cabbage is done, add some Grated Parmesan cheese, stir, then cut some corn bread, place it in a pasta dish, and cover it with the cabbage and pieces of meats. I like to mash mine all together and eat it that way. Others like to eat it piece by piece.

MANICOTTI

Shells:
5 eggs
5 cups of water
4 cups flour

Mix all together in a pan. You might need a little more flour. You want it loose but not watery, a little on the solid side. In a heated sauté pan, brush a bit of oil in pan with a small piece of paper towel. Drop about 4 to 5 tablespoonfuls of mix into pan and swirl around until it covers the bottom of pan. When the mix bubbles a bit, invert it/turn it upside down so you cook the other side for about 10-20 seconds, and layer on oiled countertop (oil it with a bit of oil and paper towel). When cooled, place in a dish that's covered with waxed paper. Separate each layer with wax paper. Makes 30 to 40-plus manicotti shells.

Annette's manicotti or lasagna filling:
2 lb. of ricotta, drain in strainer for two days in refrigerator, covered.
2 eggs
1 tsp parsley
Salt and pepper
A handful of grated mixed Romano and Parmesan cheese, more
    needed for top of sauce
1 cup of shredded mozzarella
1 cup of shredded domestic provolone cheese

Mix all together and taste for salt. Add more salt if needed. Fill each manicotti shell with 1 Tbsp of this.

Spread some marinara sauce on bottom of pan. Sprinkle mixed grated cheese on top of sauce. Place filled shells on top of sauce. Cover with more sauce so it completely covers the top. Sprinkle mixed grated cheese on top of sauce. Bake for 50 minutes, covered, in 350-degree degree oven. Serve, or let it cool down for an hour before serving.

You can freeze the stuffed shells (keeping wax paper between them), or you can completely prepare it, sauce and all, in any pan, covering it with two pieces of waxed paper on top followed with heavy-duty foil wrap. Completely or partially defrost, and bake as above.

RAVIOLI

3 to 4 cups of flour
¼ cup of olive oil
3 to 5 eggs
¼ cup of water
1 Tbsp salt

Make a well, and mix all together on a floured board or countertop.
Knead well until smooth, adding more flour as needed for easy
handling. Roll out to a thin layer.

Place filling mix by spoonfuls onto dough. Fold over each spoonful,
cut each, and close by pressing the tines of a fork on all closed sides of
each ravioli. Cook in salted boiling water that you've added a bit of olive
oil to. Homemade pasta only needs to boil for 5 to 7 minutes.

Cheese filling:
2 lb. of ricotta, drain for 2 to 3 days in strainer, refrigerated and
covered
   with Saran wrap
¾ cup of grated Romano/Parmesan cheese mix
1 egg yolk
Salt and pepper to taste
½ tsp parsley

Mix together well. Drop by spoonfuls onto rolled out pasta, and place on
floured board until ready to cook.

Boil ravioli in boiling salted water that you've drizzled a little olive
oil to. Taste water for salt, and add more salt if it needs it. Drain pasta.
Add tomato sauce. Sprinkle grated cheese on top. Serve.

GNOCCHI (Potato Pasta)

3 boiled baking potatoes (boiled for 30 minutes, covered)
1 cup of all-purpose flour
2 Tbsp salt
¼ cup of grappa (optional; if you don't have this, you might try vodka)
1 egg
Drizzle of oil

On a board or clean countertop, mash the potatoes. Add flour, salt, grappa/ vodka, egg, and drizzle of oil and knead well. Keep adding flour until it all comes together. Take pieces at a time, and roll into long lengths that are no more than ½ inch wide. Cut into 1 inch pieces, and make an indentation in each with your finger, and roll them aside as you indent each of them. Keep doing that until you finish the dough.

Remember that when you make any homemade pasta, it doesn't take that long to cook.

Boil them in boiling salted water that you've added a drizzle of olive oil to, and cook for 5 to 8 minutes. Drain. Place in a pasta bowl. Add tomato sauce. Sprinkle grated cheese and serve.

MEATLOAF, ANNETTE'S

Everyone has their own version of meatloaf. This is mine.

½ cup rice, boiled with salt and a drizzle of olive oil in water
Salt and pepper to taste
Tempo meatloaf mix
2 eggs
1 lb. ground beef
¼ cup of milk
2 strips of diced bacon
2 more strips of bacon, for top
1 clove of finely diced garlic
½ cup frozen sweet peas
¼ to ½ cup shredded or cubed cheddar, mozzarella, and provolone cheese mix

Mix Tempo mix, eggs, and milk. Add the rest of the ingredients, and mix all together. Spread in slightly oil-greased loaf pan. Add bacon slices on top. Cook at 350 degrees for 45 to 55 minutes.

You can make and add brown gravy on top or eat as is. I make the packaged Durkee's brown gravy mix, and it tastes absolutely delicious with the meatloaf, adding the gravy to each slice of meatloaf or not.

LOBSTER SPAGHETTI SAUCE

½ cup olive oil
1 diced onion
1 diced garlic
Hot red pepper flakes (optional)
16 oz Pastene kitchen-ready ground tomatoes
2 Tbsp parsley
1 or 2 live lobsters

Boil live lobsters in covered pan with water that you've added a ¼ cup of white vinegar to until the lobster turns pink. Break off the tail and clean out the middle portion of the meat. Break off the claws and legs. Cut the head off, and clean the middle too under warm water along with the body.

Sauté onion and garlic for 2 minutes or until it starts to wilt. Add 1 tablespoonful of parsley (and pepper flakes) and black pepper. Sauté for one minute. Add Kitchen-Ready Tomatoes and salt. Cook for 5 minutes. Add cleaned lobster tail, legs and body. Cook for a half hour.

Cook spaghetti in salted water with a drizzle of olive oil; drain and pour into platter. Take out lobster, letting the juices drop into the sauce, and place in a dish. Stir the sauce, pour sauce over spaghetti. Serve with lobster parts in side dish or on top of pasta.

TOMATO SAUCE (Annette's)— Avellino Style (Neapolitan Style)

Onion, diced
Garlic, diced
1 Tbsp garlic
1 tsp parsley
1 Tbsp basil
¼ tsp sage
¼ tsp rosemary
Dash of black pepper
Hot red pepper flakes (optional)
½ tsp sugar (optional, I use only when tomatoes are acidy)
½ cup olive oil
1 can Pastene kitchen-ready ground tomatoes

On medium heat, sauté onion and garlic together for 2 minutes. Add some black pepper, then the rest of the herbs, and sauté for 1 to 2 more minutes or until onions are wilted and starting to turn color. Add tomatoes. Add 1 tsp of salt and sugar, if needed. Fill the tomato can with water, filling it halfway, swooshing the water around in the can, and throw the water that's gathered any leftover tomatoes in the can into the tomato sauce. Lower heat and cook for half an hour. Taste for salt. Add more salt if it's too bland and sugar, if it's too acidy.

PESTO SAUCE

For 1 lb. of pasta

Pound to a paste, in a blender:
2 cloves of garlic
4 small bunches basil leaves or parsley ½ cup toasted pine nuts or walnuts Pinch of salt

Gradually add to the above:
3 Tbsp grated Parmesan cheese
3 tsp grated Romano cheese
¾ to 1 cup olive oil
Black pepper to taste (optional)
Red pepper flakes to taste (optional)

MEAT TOMATO SAUCE
1 lb. ground beef (85 to 93 percent less fat)
Salt to taste
2 Tbsp olive oil
¼ cup white distilled vinegar
½ tsp sugar (optional)

Boil ground beef in salted water, vinegar, olive oil, and sugar for 5 minutes. Drain.

Sauce:
Diced onion
diced garlic
1 Tbsp parsley
2 Tbsp basil
½ tsp sage
½ tsp rosemary (optional)
1 green or red pepper, diced
Black pepper for taste
Hot red pepper flakes (optional)
½ tsp sugar (optional, I use for and when tomatoes are acidy)
½ cup olive oil
1 can kitchen-ready tomatoes (I use Pastene ground tomatoes)

On medium high heat, sauté onion, garlic, and black pepper together for 2 minutes. Add the rest of the herbs and sauté for 2 more minutes. Add ground beef, salt to taste, and add a little more of the white distilled vinegar. Mix and cook for 1 minute. Taste the meat for salt, and add more salt if it needs for taste. Add ½ cup of the kitchen-ready, salt to taste and sugar (optional – if needed). Cook for 1 more minute. Add the rest of the tomatoes. Rinse the tomato can with water, filling it a quarter of the way. Swirl the water around the can, and pour the water into the meat sauce. Lower heat and cook for 1 hour or until ground beef is tender. Taste for salt. Add more salt if it's too bland. If the tomatoes are acidy, add a teaspoon of sugar to take the acid taste away.

TOMATO SAUCE for Eggplant Parmigiana

1 diced onion
1 diced garlic
2 Tbsp basil
1 tsp parsley
½ tsp oregano
¼ tsp black pepper
Red pepper flakes
½ tsp sugar
1 tsp salt
½ cup olive oil
16 oz. can Pastene kitchen-ready tomatoes

Sauté onion and garlic for 2 minutes on medium high heat until the onions *start* to wilt. Add the rest of the herbs except for sugar and salt. Sauté for 1 more minute. Add the salt and sugar to the can of kitchen-ready tomatoes. Add tomatoes to herbed oil and spices. Fill half of the empty tomato can with water, and swish the water around the inside until all the leftover tomatoes are into the water. Add to tomato sauce. Lower heat and cook for 30 minutes. Taste for salt.

No matter how one fries their eggplants, it's the tomato sauce and fresh breadcrumbs that actually make the eggplant parmigiana taste great along with a good-tasting Romano cheese that's sprinkled over the sauce as you layer your eggplants.

EGGPLANT PARMIGIANA, Annette's
(One of my constantly asked-for recipes.)
Eggplant Tomato Sauce (Page 121 or sauce on page 118)

2 eggplants, washed and patted dry

Cut eggplants, either round or lengthwise, and leave on board covered with cloth or paper towels to dry for at least 4 to 5 hours or overnight. Don't cut them too thick or too thin, about 1/3 inch thickness or a bit less should be good.

¾ cup of vegetable oil
¼ cup of olive oil

Mix both of them together and use to spread a little at a time on baking sheet or use in frying pan.

Shredded mozzarella and domestic provolone cheese, mixed together (I either buy whole pieces and shred my own or bag mixes of both cheeses.)

In first bowl:
Add 4 cups *fresh* Italian bread crumbs, 1 Tbsp parsley, ½ cup each of Romano and Parmigiano grated cheese, salt and pepper to taste.

In second bowl:
Beat 5 to 7 eggs (depending on how many eggplant pieces you have) with ¼ cup each of grated Romano and Parmigiano cheese; salt and pepper to taste.

You can either fry or bake the eggplants. I prefer baked—they're just as delicious, and you get it done faster. Preheat oven to 450 degrees.

While the oven is heating up, dip the eggplants in the beaten eggs mixture and then in breadcrumb mix. Layer them in a dish. Dribble some oil on the baking sheet so it slightly covers the bottom of the sheet. Add as many eggplant slices that you can fit. Bake for 10 minutes on each side. Place on dish covered with paper towels. Place cooked eggplants in this dish. Drizzle more oil on baking sheet and repeat cooking time and layers until you finish cooking all the eggplant slices.

Pour some of the tomato sauce on bottom of pan. Add eggplant slices.
Sprinkle some of the shredded cheese combo on top of each eggplant.
Add some tomato sauce on each slice. Sprinkle Romano/Grated Parmesan cheese on top of sauce. Continue layering the eggplants the same way until finished. The top layer should have a lot more sauce all over. Sprinkle with a good amount of the grated Romano/Parmesan cheeses or if you prefer, just grated Romano instead of the mix.

Cover and bake at 350 degrees for 45 minutes.

RICE WITH MEAT SAUCE

Make meat sauce (page 120).

Heat 2 cups of water till it comes to a boil. Add 1 tsp of salt, a little olive oil, and 1 cup of jasmine rice or whatever rice you prefer. Stir and cover. Lower heat to simmer. Cook covered for 30 minutes, no more than 30 minutes. Drain and spray cool water over all. Place in dish, add grated cheese and/or diced/shredded mozzarella and provolone cheese mix, and stir together well. Add half of the meat sauce and stir. Add and stir in the rest of the meat sauce. You don't have to add the shredded cheeses to make it tasty. It's delicious with or without it. Taste for salt. You can make this with plain sauce too.

PASTA E FAGIOLI (Pasta with Beans)

I normally use the white kidney beans for this, or I cook fresh beans in a lot of water that you keep adding as the beans swell and get tender. Season the bean water and boil them with olive oil, 1 bay leaf, and salt and pepper to taste.

Pasta: ditalini, or elbows White kidney beans

Sauce:
1 garlic clove, diced
1 onion, diced
A little each of red pepper flakes, basil, mint, and fresh rosemary
½ cup olive oil
8 oz. of kitchen-ready tomatoes or ½ can of the 16 oz. can (Pastene)
½ can of water
Salt and pepper to taste

Fry the garlic and onion until it starts to wilt. Add red pepper, black pepper, basil, mint, and fresh rosemary and cook for 1 more minute. Add the tomatoes, water, and salt. Cook for 20 minutes and taste for salt. If the tomatoes taste a bit acidy, add a half teaspoon of sugar (sugar takes the acidity away). Cook for another 10 minutes.

Cook the pasta. When the water comes to a boil, add the pasta, salt, and a drizzle of oil in the water. Boil for 8 minutes or until al dente. Add the beans and cook for another 3 to 5 minutes. Drain ¾ of the water from the pasta. Add the tomato sauce to the pasta. Sprinkle some grated parmesan cheese and serve with additional grated cheese and red pepper flakes at the table.

PASTA, POTATOES AND PEAS
Easy and delicious.

If you have any leftover sauce without meat, you can make this meal easily, and it will always be delicious! If you don't have any leftover sauce, then just make a small amount of regular tomato sauce (page 118).

1 can of sweet peas
½ to 1 lb. of medium-sized pasta shells or pasta of your choice
1 large potato, cut in thirds, and then sideways, by ½ inch pieces 1 Tbsp salt
Tomato sauce (page 118) or 1 cup of leftover tomato sauce Grated Parmesan or Romano cheese

Make your sauce. Let it cook for 30 minutes and set aside. Bring a pan filled ¾ of the way up with water. When it comes to boil, add at least 1 tablespoon of salt, a drizzle of olive oil, pasta and the diced potato. Let it cook for 5 minutes. Taste for salt and add a little more if it's not tasty. Drain ¾ of the water from the pan. Add the tomato sauce and grated cheese. Mix well. Serve with a dish of grated cheese for those who want to add more cheese.

SPANISH RICE CASSEROLE

½ cup uncooked rice
6 strips of bacon, cut in pieces
½ lb ground beef
1 medium onion, finely diced
Salt and pepper to taste
2 cups kitchen-ready tomatoes
Tabasco sauce or red pepper flakes (optional)

Place bacon in frying pan with onion, ground beef, and dry rice. Cook until meat and rice are golden brown. Add tomatoes, salt, and pepper. Cover tightly. Simmer for 1 hour or until rice is tender. Add more water if needed.

STUFFED ARTICHOKES

4 artichokes

Clean artichokes by taking the small leaves off the bottom. Cut straight across the top, taking off the thorned tops. Clip the rest of the thorns off the rest of the side leaves. Cut off about a half inch of the bottom stem evenly so it can stand on its own. Open up the middle and side leaves a little. Soak them in water for 20 minutes. Drain and shake the water out of them.

Stuffing:
2 cups of bread crumbs
½ cup grated Romano and Parmesan cheese combo
1 finely diced garlic
Salt and pepper to taste
3 Tbsp olive oil
Enough water to just moisten the breadcrumb mixture.

Mix all together well. Taste for salt and cheese. If it's tasty, you're all set. If it's not, add a little more salt and/or cheese. Stuff each side artichoke leaves all over. In a big enough pan to hold the 4 artichokes standing up, add 2 cups of water, ¼ cup of olive oil, 1 Tbsp salt, 3 crushed cloves of garlic, and 1 Tbsp of oregano. Stir. Cover and cook for about 1 hour. Check at half hour interval for water evaporation add some more if it needs it.

Unless your artichokes are old and tough, they usually cook in one hour. If they're tough, let them cook another 10 or 15 minutes or more by testing one leaf.

FAVA BEANS in Light Tomato Sauce

1 bag of cleaned fava beans
½ cup of olive oil
1 large sliced onion, sweet
Black pepper
½ tsp oregano
Salt to taste

Sauté onion for 2 minutes in olive oil with pepper and oregano. Add fava beans and cook for 10 minutes, stirring on and off. Add ¼ cup of tomatoes. Add 1 cup of water. Add salt to taste. Stir and cover, stirring on and off until the water has almost all absorbed but is still juicy. You can either sop bread with this or eat alone.

PASTIERI (Spaghetti Pie)—Appetizer

1 lb. ricotta cheese
Salt and pepper to taste
2 eggs
1 lb. thin spaghetti
Raisins (optional)
Sausages or ham (optional) (try some diced up ham and/or sausages
    in small pieces – I don't use, I like it plain and delicious)
¼ cup olive oil (just covering the bottom of pan)

Boil spaghetti in salted water for 8 minutes or until al dente. Drain. In a dish, mix ricotta, salt and pepper, and 2 eggs. Add raisins and meats if you like. Mix well. Add to spaghetti and mix well.

Pour in a frying pan that's covered with olive oil on the bottom of a nonstick pan. Cover pan and shake lightly on and off so it doesn't stick to bottom of pan. Cook on medium heat for 8 to 10 minutes. Invert pan and turn spaghetti pie over and cook the other side for 8 to 10 more minutes. Each side should shake loosely. Add a bit more oil if it's sticky. Both sides should be a little brownish when done. Remove and place in a dish. Eat warm or cool at room temperature or keep in refrigerator until ready to eat.

STUFFED BRASCIOLE

Have your butcher or meat center cut you some beef or pork meat for brasciole - have him/her tenderize each piece. When you get them home and are ready to make the brasciole, beat each cutlet with a meat tenderizer again. Lay each cutlet and sprinkle over each cutlet the following in this order:

Salt
Pepper
Mint
Basil
Parsley
Oregano
Onion, finely diced
Garlic, finely diced
Grated cheese
Olive oil, drizzled on top of ingredients

Roll it like a jelly roll and hold together with white thread around each brasciola. Fry in olive oil until lightly browned, and add to your tomato sauce.

You can also add any other ingredient that you feel is more to your taste with the above ingredients.

This sauce, along with sausages in the sauce, makes a delicious sauce for Lasagna. The ingredients between the 2 meats adds a special flavor to the sauce.

MEATBALLS (Annette's)

2 lbs ground beef, chuck or 85 percent or 87 percent sirloin
½ lb. ground pork (optional)
½ cup of grated Parmesan cheese
½ cup of grated Romano cheese
1Tbsp of basil, crushed
1 tsp of parsley
¼ tsp of sage
Pinch of oregano
¼ tsp of rosemary (optional)
¼ cup of olive oil
4 to 5 eggs for moisture and keeping together (if the mix is too dry, add another egg)
1-1½ cups fresh breadcrumbs moistened with water *'til just moistened*
1 Tbsp salt
½ tsp black pepper

Mix all together well. If it's too hard or dry, add another egg. In a frying pan with ½ cup of olive oil, drop a small teaspoonful of the mixture and cook on both sides. Taste to see if it needs more salt. If it tastes good, roll the rest of the mixture by spoonfuls in the palm of your hands into round meatballs and fry. You can also freeze these in a double bag for use at a later time.

STUFFED MUSHROOMS (Annette's)

Separate mushroom stems from caps from 1 pkg of mushrooms. Dice stems and save. Boil mushroom caps in salted water for 1 minute. Remove with slotted spoon. Don't throw the water away. Boil diced mushroom stems in that salted water for 15 seconds and drain saving some of the water for the stuffing.

Filling:
2 cups of fresh Italian plain breadcrumbs Boiled mushroom stem pieces
¼ cup of grated Romano cheese
1 finely diced garlic
Salt and pepper to taste
A little olive oil

½ tsp parsley
¼ cup of the boiled mushroom water 1 egg

Mix all together. Taste for salt. Stuff mushrooms.

Place on a cookie sheet with salted water mixed with a little olive oil on bottom of pan. Bake at 350 degrees for 20 to 30 minutes or until tops look cooked.

STUFFED ZUCCHINI

Preheat oven to 350 degrees.

2 medium young zucchini (*in other words, don't buy the ones that are full grown and have tough seeds*), cut in half

1½ cups fresh bread crumbs
½ cup grated Romano cheese
Olive oil
Middle portion of zucchinis, cut up and boiled in salted water, and drained 1 Small Zucchini or the ends of the zucchini cut up and boiled in salted
   water and drained—reserving a bit of the water
Salt and pepper to taste
Pine nuts (optional) or any other type of nut you prefer
Raisins (optional)

Cut off about half an inch of each zucchini's head (the beginning portion of each zucchini) and then cut off the end of each zucchini at the portion where the zucchini starts to narrow down again. Cut each zucchini in half and spoon out the middle part, cut it up, and place in a bowl. Parboil the zucchini halves in salted water until they're al dente— about 2 minutes in boiling water. Cut off and dice the rest of the end portion of each zucchini until you feel the rest of the zucchini is not tender anymore. (Boil these diced pieces in salted water after you have parboiled the zucchini halves for about 2 minutes covered and 5 minutes uncovered.)

In a bowl, add breadcrumbs, grated cheese, some olive oil, salt, and pepper (and nuts) and a little of the boiled zucchini water. Add the boiled zucchini pieces. Taste for salt and cheese and add more if needed. Place in the middle of each zucchini half. In a baking dish, sprinkle some olive oil and a bit of water and salt just so it slightly covers the bottom of the dish. Place stuffed zucchini in dish and bake at 350 degrees covered for 20 to 35 minutes covered and uncovered until the top of the filling is slightly browned.

TERIYAKI SIRLOIN TIPS OR CHICKEN (Annette's)

You better triple and quadruple this recipe because it goes so fast you won't know what hit you. Even if you have any leftovers, they'll be eaten up by nightfall or the next day.

Sirloin Tips or Chicken Wings, with tips stripped of fat and cut in
    thin/thick pieces as you like it.
Duck Sauce (I keep the duck sauce from Chinese food orders) *or* World
Harbors Maui Mountain *sweet-and-sour* sauce
World Harbors/Maui Mountain *Teriyaki* Marinade
Garlic Salt
Salt
Deep dish for each of the meats

Marinate tips and chicken three days ahead: *Sometimes I like to parboil my chicken for 5 to 7 minutes so I don't have to wait so long for the chicken to cook when I grill it.* Cut sirloin tips in slices in whatever thickness you prefer. I partially freeze them for easier handling.

On the bottom of your deep dish, sprinkle garlic salt and salt. Layer tips in dish. Sprinkle salt and garlic salt over all. Sprinkle a little duck sauce a little here and there. Pour teriyaki sauce here and there, not completely covering them. Keep adding and marinating in the same way until you finish the layers of meat and/or chicken. Cover and refrigerate until ready to BBQ. For chicken, place your chicken in a deep plastic container with tight cover. Turn the container upside down each day so the marinade marinates all of the chicken pieces. They're delicious cold too!

Preheat your grill. BBQ your chicken wings until cooked. Cut one of them open to make sure it's cooked before placing in a serving dish. For sirloin Tips, BBQ for no longer than 2 minutes on each side, depending on the thickness, on high heat. If you sliced the meat thinly, then cook for not more than 1 minute on each side on high heat. Taste test one of them before removing to serving dish. You shouldn't need any additional salt, but if it tastes like it can use some more salt, sprinkle some while they're on the grill or in the serving dish.

RICE PILAF

1 cup jasmine rice or whatever long rice you like
½ cup thin egg noodles, crushed

Mix both of them together.

Mix together:
2 cups of hot water
6 to 9 cubes of Herb-Ox chicken or any brand chicken soup cubes. Stir until melted. It should taste just slightly salty. If it tastes just right, add 1 more cube. Stir before adding to rice mixture.

1 small to medium onion, diced
1 clove of garlic, diced fine
1 tsp parsley
¼ cup of vegetable oil
2 Tbsp butter

On medium heat, sauté the onion and garlic in oil and butter for about 2 minutes or until the onions start to wilt. Add parsley and sauté for another ½ minute, stirring on and off. Add the rice/noodle mixture, and stir on and off until the onion becomes just slightly light brown. Pour the stirred chicken stock all over. Stir and cover tightly. Lower heat to simmer; simmer for 30 minutes covered. Fluff and serve.

POTATO CROQUETTES
This recipe will make enough for two people.

2 large Idaho baking potatoes (with dark thick skin)
¼ cup grated Romano cheese
½ tsp parsley
Salt and pepper to taste
1 Tbsp butter
1 egg, beaten
Domestic slices of provolone cheese cut into 1½ inch lengths

In a Dish: 2 eggs beaten by themselves

On a paper towel: 1½ to 2 cups of plain *fresh* Italian breadcrumbs or more if needed

Boil potatoes on medium high heat for 30 minutes in a covered pan. Stick a fork into the potato to see if they're cooked. Drain. Cool until you're able to handle them so you can peel the skin off.

In a bowl, place the butter piece on bottom. Place the peeled potatoes on top. Add the grated cheese, salt (about 1 teaspoon or more), pepper, parsley, and beaten egg. Mash potatoes with a potato masher, mixing everything together well. Taste a piece of it and see if it needs more salt. Roll a spoonful of the potato mix in your hands to make a thick-like stick, about 3 to 4 inches long or as long or short as you want them. Make an indentation in the middle. Place a piece of the provolone cheese in the middle. Gather the sides of the potato onto the cheese, and roll in your hand to close it up.

Roll the croquette in the beaten eggs, and then in the bread crumbs. Place in a dish. Cover with wax paper and refrigerate at least 2 to 3 hours before frying. Preheat oil on medium high heat. Let each side fry for about 1 minute or until lightly brown. Check the bottom to see if it's turned a nice light brown color. Cook on all sides. Place on a dish covered with paper towel. Cool and eat.

LASAGNA

Boil 4 Italian sweet sausages for 7 to 8 minutes

Make the tomato sauce (page 118). Place the sausages in the sauce and cook for 1½ hours. The sausages will give the sauce an added flavor. If you enjoy brasciole (page 131), you can make at least 1 and add it to the sauce to give it a very special flavor for the lasagna. It does make a difference.

Filling:
3 lbs of ricotta (or more if you want it cheesy), drained in a plastic
    drainer for 2 days.
1 tsp parsley
A little black pepper
1 tsp salt
3 eggs, beaten
Shredded mozzarella/provolone mix – ¾ cup of each
    Grated Romano cheese, a good handful

In a bowl, mix all of the above together. Taste for salt. Set aside.

Boil: 1 lb. lasagna noodles in salted (1 tablespoonful of salt) water with a little olive oil for 8 minutes. Before draining, taste the water for salt and add more if needed. Drain the noodles. Run cold water over them so you can handle them.

In a lasagna pan, add tomato sauce on bottom, grated Romano cheese, than layer noodles. Add 1/3 of the filling, top with some more sauce, sprinkle grated cheese over sauce. Keep repeating the layers until you finish. End with noodles on top. Add more sauce over noodles. Sprinkle a good amount of grated cheese. Cover with aluminum foil and bake for 1 hour at 350 degrees. Cook this ahead so it will have time to settle.

WHITE LASAGNA

(This does not require tomato sauce.)

1 pkg. sliced mushrooms
½ onion, diced
¼ cup olive oil and a bit of butter
white wine
Pine nuts
½ tsp parsley
½ tsp oregano
Salt and pepper to taste

Sauté the mushrooms and onions in oil (and butter) for 2 minutes. Add wine and herbs. Toss in pine nuts. Layer on top of ricotta filling and keep layering until finished.

Cover with aluminum foil and bake 45-60 minutes.

FRIED OR BAKED FISH of Any Type

In a Ziploc bag, add flour, salt, and pepper. Shake. Rinse fish. Place in bag and shake. Take them out one at a time, and fry in preheated vegetable oil and olive oil mix.

Baked Fish Fillets: Haddock, Cod, Stuffed Fillets, etc.
If you want to bake fillets, place in pan or dish with a little bit of oil or butter on bottom of pan. Sprinkle salt and some parsley on bottom of pan. Layer the fish and sprinkle each with salt, pepper, and parsley. Top crushed Ritz crackers all over fillets. Drizzle a little olive oil or vegetable oil all over topping. Bake at 400 degrees for 15 to 18 minutes. If you cook it any longer than that, it will be dry.

Shelled Fish: Calamari, Thin Fillets, Clams, Scallops, Shrimps, etc.
In a dish or Ziploc bag, add flour, salt, and pepper to taste and 1 Tbsp fine corn flour. Mix well. Add fish and shake well so that they're completely coated. Fry for no more than 2 minutes on each side or keep turning (calamari) until nice and yellowish. Shrimps: once they turn pink, they're done. If you keep frying them, they'll be dry.

Fresh Water Fish: Strippers, Bass, etc.
If you cook them whole, clean the insides, place on aluminum foil that has been sprinkled with Mrs. Dash original, salt, pepper, 1 Tbsp parsley, and place fish on this. Sprinkle the same thing in the fish's cavity and on top of the fish. Sprinkle with some oil (olive or corn oil). Close the foil together, and cook on grill for 10 to 15 minutes at 400 degrees or 15 to 20 minutes on 300 degrees and 15 to 20 minutes in a 400-degree oven. You can fillet the fish and just add the spices and oil on top, still in an aluminum foil sheet closed up.

STEAK FISH WITH TOMATOES

1 onion, diced
1 garlic, diced
1 tsp basil
½ cup kitchen-ready tomatoes or fresh tomatoes
Oregano

Fry onions and garlic in oil until wilted. Add basil and fry for 1 minute. Add tomatoes and season with salt. Add fish steak on top of tomatoes, and sprinkle some oregano on top of fish with salt. Cook for 5 minutes. Turn fish to cook on other side. Taste for salt and serve.

CODFISH CASSEROLE
Preheat oven to 350 degrees.

3 strips of bacon (optional)
1 fresh or 1 pkg. frozen codfish
5 medium baking potatoes
1 medium onion, finely chopped
1 Tbsp butter or oil
¼ cup milk
¼ cup fresh Italian bread crumbs
¼ cup grated Parmesan cheese
Salt and pepper to taste

Fry bacon, saving fat. Cook codfish in boiling water about 7 minutes and drain. Cook potatoes for 30 minutes in covered pan. Mash with butter, milk, salt, and pepper. Add codfish to the potato mix. Add some oil, about ¼ cup, and mix again. Put in lightly oil-greased casserole dish. Sprinkle bread crumbs and grated cheese on top. Bake for 30 minutes at 350 degrees.

This recipe may be made in advance and may also be frozen if made with fresh fish.

SHRIMP SCAMPI with Rice or Angel Hair Pasta

1 lb. shrimps, de-shelled and deveined

3 cloves garlic, diced
1 Tbsp parsley
¼ to ½ tsp of hot red pepper flakes (optional)
¼ tsp black pepper
1 lemon, juiced (optional)
Salt for taste
6 to 8 pieces of marinated artichoke hearts (optional)
¾ -1 cup of extra virgin or regular olive oil
¾ -1 lb. of angel hair pasta **or**
1-1½ cups of jasmine rice, precooked with2-3 cups of salted water and a
    bit of olive oil

Sauté the garlic, hot pepper flakes (optional), black pepper, (and lemon juice) into the olive oil for about 1 minute or until the garlic starts to just wilt. (Add artichoke hearts. Cook for 2 minutes.) Add shrimps and sprinkle salt for taste (at least 1 tsp) and cook until they turn pink and plumpy. Taste for salt. Remove from heat.

Cook angel hair spaghetti or rice in salted water with a little bit of olive oil. If you're cooking spaghetti, take ½ cup of the boiled salted water before draining spaghetti and add to shrimp sauce (optional).

Drain the pasta or rice. Place in pasta dish. Add ½ of the shrimp sauce and stir well. Add the rest of the shrimp sauce on top and serve. Have grated cheese on the table for those who wish to use it along with red pepper flakes. Delicious with or without grated cheese.

PIZZA GHIENA—Easter Filled Pie
(A meal in itself.)
Heat oven to 400 degrees.

Crust:
2 cups of flour
Salt and pepper to taste
2 Tbsp of olive oil
3 eggs

Mix together and knead until smooth. If the dough is too stiff, add another egg. Let stand for 10 minutes. Cut into 2 pieces. Roll one piece out to fit bottom of a deep 9- or 10-inch pan making it thicker than the top piece. Roll the second piece, and save for top to place on top of filling.

Filling:
1 whole ½ lb piece of boiled baked ham, diced
1 whole piece of dry Sopressata Sausage, diced
1 fresh ricotta cheese, cut up
8 to 12 eggs
1 lb. ricotta, drain for 2 days before using
Pepper to taste—maybe 1½ tsp
1 cup of grated Parmesan cheese
½ cup of grated Romano cheese
Prosciutto piece, diced (I don't use)

(Do not use salt with this recipe. The ham and sausage and grated cheeses will have enough salt to give it taste.) You may also add any other dried type of meat to this recipe.

Mix well until all are well incorporated with all the ingredients. It should be slightly wet. Pour into crust. Place top layer, fold and pinch sides under to close it up.

Place toothpicks on top of top crust layer, three down and two across at the center, making a slit with each so that air can escape as it cooks.

Bake at 400 degrees for 20 minutes. Lower oven to 350 degrees, and bake for 1 hour more or until you see juices coming out from the top of the crust. You might have to wiggle the toothpicks up, down, and sideways - to make sure that their openings are not closed—to let the air escape.

STUFFED PEPPERS

Wash the outside and clear the inside of seeds.

Filling:
2 cups of *fresh* Italian Bread Crumbs
¾ tsp Parsley
1 Clove of Garlic, diced/minced
Salt and Pepper to taste
¾ cup Grated Parmesan Cheese
¾ cup Grated Romano Cheese
Raisins (optional) Pine nuts (optional)
¼ cup of Olive Oil
Sirloin or Ground Chuck beef, boiled in salted water and
    rinsed clear (optional)
¾ cup of Rice, boiled in 1 Cup of salted water with a bit of olive oil
    for 30 minutes (optional)
2 Eggs
¼ cup of Water
½ can or 8 oz of Pastene Ground Kitchen Ready Tomatoes

Mix all together except for the water and kitchen-ready tomatoes.
Taste for salt. The filling should be just moist but on the drier side
rather than wet side. Fill peppers. Fry filled peppers in a pan of olive
oil (about ½ cup or so that the oil is enough to coat the bottom of the
pan.) Cook for about 2 minutes on each side. Turn the peppers upside
down too when frying. Add tomatoes. Add ½ tsp salt to tomatoes, add
the water, and stir around peppers. Cover and cook for 30 to 45
minutes. If you want to make more and freeze them, after cooking
them on each side, add the tomatoes, water, and salt. Cook for 1
minute and place in pan. Cover tightly and freeze until ready to use.
When you defrost them, cook them for 30 to 45 minutes like you would
as if you had just made them.

You may also add whatever else you desire to this filling.

MY MOTHER'S CORN BREAD

My mother got us addicted to this meal. It's simple yet delicious and hearty. We love this bread by itself or crushed into cooked cabbage and pork with garlic, oil, and some hot meat or spice.

2 cups fine corn flour or meal
½ cup regular flour
1 handful of grated Parmesan cheese
1 handful of grated Romano cheese
A good swizzle of olive oil
½ cup of warm water
Salt and pepper to taste
Frying pan coated with olive oil
Sausages, fried bacon pieces, pepperoni pieces (optional additions)

Put all ingredients into a bowl. Add more warm water to make it moist but not loose. Taste for salt and cheese. It should taste good to the fingertip. Put into oiled frying pan. Spread the mix evenly into pan, and push the sides into the center with a fork so you're lifting the mix from the wall of the frying pan. Brush a little more warm water on top of the leveled mix. Cover and let it cook on top of the stove for about 15 to 20 minutes on medium heat. Slightly shake the pan every once in a while so it stays loose on the bottom. Once it's formed a crust on the bottom of the corn bread (you can lift a corner with a spatula or fork to check for the crust), invert the corn bread onto a larger dish or flip over into the pan. Add a little more olive oil in the frying pan if it doesn't have any. Place the uncooked side of the corn bread into the pan, and let it cook for another 20 minutes or so until a crust is formed at the bottom.

You should have a nice crust on the top and bottom of the bread. This can be a meal in itself and delicious or cut up and eaten with cabbage and pork meat mixture.

Hope you enjoy it as much as we do.

ZUCCHINI TOMATO CIAMBOTTA

2 Zucchinis, sliced in half, then in 1/3 lengths in strip style
1 Large Sweet Onion, sliced
¼ cup of Olive Oil
¼ cup of Pastene Kitchen-Ready Tomatoes or 2 crushed fresh tomatoes
Salt to taste

Place zucchini in olive oil and cook for 5 minutes (3 minutes if you like the zucchini crunchy). Add sliced onions and salt to taste. Cook until both are cooked and wilted. Add tomatoes and ¼ cup of water. Cook until water almost absorbs. Remove from heat. Taste for salt.

Sop with Italian bread or eat as is as a vegetable side dish.

CHICKEN PARMIGIANA
Preheat oven to 350 degrees.

1 pkg. shredded mozzarella/provolone cheese tomato sauce, Avellino style (page 118 but add green diced peppers to the sauce)
12 or more breaded and fried chicken cutlets (page 107)
Grated Parmesan-and-Romano cheese mix

Make your tomato sauce and set aside.

In an aluminum foil pan or lasagna dish pan, pour sauce on bottom of pan. Sprinkle some grated cheese over sauce. Layer chicken cutlets. Add some mozzarella/provolone shredded cheese on each cutlet. Pour some tomato sauce over most of the cheese and cutlet but not covering the cutlet. Sprinkle with grated Romano cheese. Keep layering until you finish. Add the rest of the tomato sauce on top, and add some of the mozzarella/ provolone mix followed by grated cheese. Cover with aluminum foil.
Bake for 45 to 60 minutes.

VEGETABLES

Broccoli Rabe

Cut stems off until you come to the tender portion of each rabe piece. If the rabe is young, then just cut a little off at the bottom. Wash and put aside. Put a cup of water into a deep pan. Add the washed rabe and cook covered for 7 minutes. Drain and place in serving dish. Fry 3 or 4 crushed pieces of garlic in olive oil until they turn pinkish/brownish color. You may also fry, with the garlic, dried sweet or hot peppers. Remove from heat. Salt the rabe and sprinkle the oil/garlic mixture over the rabe and toss until completely blended. Taste for salt and serve.

Savoy Cabbage

Cut the core and first leaves off the head of the cabbage. Rinse the cabbage head underwater. Take off the first two rows of cabbage leaves, wash, and cut them in half. Quarter the rest of the head, cutting and taking off the core of the cabbage. Pull them apart and boil in a pan of water—about 2 cups of water—for 15 to 20 minutes. Drain and set aside. Fry 3 or 4 crushed pieces of garlic in olive oil until they turn pinkish/brownish color. Remove from heat. Salt the cabbage and sprinkle the oil/garlic mixture over this and toss until completely blended. Taste for salt and serve.

Spinach

Cut some of the stem off the spinach and discard any old, wilted leaves. Wash the spinach in a clean sink filled with enough water to wash the amount of spinach you are going to cook, and wash two or three times until no dirt appears on the bottom of the sink, placing the spinach leaves in a strainer each time you rinse them. You can either parboil the leaves and have it as a salad with oil and a squeezed lemon, salted to taste, or you can fry some garlic cloves in olive oil, like above, until lightly browned. Pour over parboiled spinach, salt to taste and serve.

I like my vegetables in garlic and oil: Sauté crushed or diced garlic (as many as you want)—I use 4 to 6 cloves of garlic—until lightly browned. When the garlic starts to turn color, add some red pepper flakes (optional). When I serve my vegetables just plain boiled, I let my guests season it as they want with salt, oil, and/or lemon or vinegar.

POLE BEANS in Tomato Sauce

½ cup Pastene kitchen-ready or 2 diced tomatoes, crushed by hand
1 tsp of mint
¼ tsp of black pepper
1 small onion, diced
1 clove of garlic, diced
2 lb. of pole or wide beans
½ cup of olive oil
1 tsp salt
1 cup of water

Wash beans. Put aside.

In a deep pan, add olive oil, onion, and garlic and sauté until wilted. Add black pepper and mint. Sauté for 1 minute. Add tomatoes, water and 1 tsp salt. Cook for 5 minutes. Add beans and cook until tender. Taste for salt. Add more water if it starts to dry up. You want enough water left in there to make a bit of a sauce for sopping or spooning over beans.

SWEET OLIVE OIL QUICK BREAD
Preheat oven to 350 degrees

2½ cups flour
2 tsp baking powder
1 pinch salt
1 cup sugar
2 eggs, lightly beaten
¾ cup milk
½ cup extra virgin olive oil
½ cup golden raisins
1 grated lemon peel
¼ cup pine nuts

Stir flour, baking powder, salt, and sugar. Add eggs, milk, and olive oil and mix well. Toss raisins in some flour, coating them. Add grated lemon peel and toss again. Add to mixture. Grease and flour pan/loaf pan. Smooth top of batter surface. Sprinkle pine nuts all over. Bake for 55 minutes or until toothpick comes out clean in center.

OLIVE LOAF BREAD, Annette's
Preheat oven to 325 degrees.

4 cups flour
1 Tbsp salt or sea salt
black pepper for taste
20 green queen olives, sliced from pits and diced into different cuts
20 black cured olives, sliced from pits and diced into different cuts 1 cup shredded four-cheese mix
1 cup shredded domestic provolone cheese
½ cup grated Romano cheese of good quality
½ cup virgin olive oil or olive oil
1 egg
¼ cup milk
1 Tbsp rosemary, crushed

Mix all together and place on floured board, kneading until it comes all together into a soft dough. Let it rest to double its size. Knead again and break apart into half. Knead each, place in oil-greased loaves, and let it rest until it doubles in size. Make a slit on top. Mix 1/3 cup olive oil, grated cheese, salt, and crushed rosemary in a small dish. Mix well and brush on top of loaves after they have risen. Bake for 1 hour or until you see sides and top become light brown.

You may also add nuts to this if you wish.

PIZZA

4 cups unbleached flour
1 Tbsp salt
1 tbsp dry yeast
1 Tbsp sugar or 2 Tbsp honey
1 cup lukewarm water
1 egg (optional)
¼ cup extra virgin olive oil or regular olive oil
4 Tbsp milk (I don't use)

Place yeast in a coffee mug and add sugar/honey and olive oil and mix. Add *lukewarm* water and stir. Let it rise—this will take about 2-4 minutes. In the meantime, in a deep bowl, add flour, salt, (egg), and milk. Add water mix, and mix well, adding more flour until it's not sticky to your hands but tender. Knead on floured board or clean countertop. Sprinkle some olive oil in bowl and place dough in it turning it so it wets all sides. Sprinkle some flour over this. Cover and let it rise. Punch down and let it rise again.

Preheat oven to 410 or 425 degrees if you like crunchy dough.

Roll out on floured board/countertop to the shape of your pan. Sprinkle a little olive oil in pan and spread oil all over with your hand. Add dough to pan, spreading dough on and off as it rises until it reaches and stays to the edges. Spread sauce, then sprinkle mozzarella/provolone shredded cheese mix all over, then whatever else you want on your pizza, sprinkle olive oil here and there and bake in preheated 425 degree oven for 16-18 minutes on lower or middle oven level.

PIZZA SAUCE

I like my sauce on the light side.

8 oz. can Crushed Tomatoes OR slice up 1 or 2 tomatoes and layer them on the dough here and there or cut and crush them by hand.
½ tsp Salt
1 Small Garlic clove, finely diced
1 to 2 tsp Sugar *(you might not need it if your tomatoes are sweet and not acidy or if you use the fresh sliced tomatoes)*
¼ to ½ cup Olive Oil
¼ tsp Oregano
Fresh basil, cut up
Black pepper to taste
Red Pepper flakes (optional)
A handful of Parmesan grated cheese (optional)

Sauce: In a small deep pan, sauté garlic for 1 minute in olive oil. Add oregano and black pepper. Add tomatoes, sugar, and salt. Add water and stir. Taste for salt and acidity. If it tastes acidy, add some more sugar. Sometimes, the tomatoes are acidy unless you use fresh tomatoes. Cool before spreading on pizza.
OR
I like to put everything in a blender and then spread the sauce on the pizza dough, add provolone/mozzarella shredded cheese and sprinkle olive oil here and there. Bake for 16-18 minutes. Check the crust at 15 minutes so you don't overcook it.

CANASCIONE—Cheese Turnovers (for Christmas and Easter)
This is a recipe from all around the outskirts of Frosinone and San Donato, Italy
Preheat oven to 375 degrees.

Filling:
2 lb. Ricotta—drained for 2 days
Fresh cheese (optional), cut up
2 cups grated Parmesan cheese
1 cup grated Romano cheese
1 Tbsp black pepper
1 tsp parsley
5 to 8 eggs

Mix all together in a bowl. Taste for salt. With all the grated cheese that this recipe uses, you shouldn't need any salt at all. But in case you do, add ½ tsp at a time. Put aside or refrigerate until you're ready with the dough.

Dough:
6 cups of flour
3 tsp salt
1 Tbsp black pepper
5 eggs
¼ cup olive oil
½ cup Crisco

On a floured board, make a well with the flour and add all the ingredients in the middle. Mix with a fork, gathering the flour into the well little by little until you have it all together. Knead. Add more flour or eggs to get a soft consistency enough to roll out easily with your rolling pin. Once you have that consistency, let it sit for about 30 minutes, covered with a paper towel or clean cloth. Cut your dough into thirds or fourths. Roll each piece out, more widthwise than lengthwise. Widthwise because you're going to put a good tablespoonful of the filling in each section of the dough, leaving enough room at the top to cover the filling, cutting around it and making it into somewhat of a turnover. Hopefully, you'll have rolled the dough out thin enough to get two rows of fillings for each piece or more. Place on ungreased baking sheet.

In a small dish, beat one egg with some milk. Brush over each turnover, and bake in a 375-degree preheated oven for 30 to 40 minutes or until golden brown. If you see the cheese swell out of some of the turnovers, that's okay.

CALZONE, Annette's
Preheat oven to 350 degrees.

1 pizza dough or frozen bread dough, defrosted
½ lb turkey ham
½ lb boiled ham or low salt ham
5 breakfast sausages (I like the maple flavored)
6 pieces of cooked bacon
3 boiled eggs, sliced

Cook your bacon, but not to a crisp, in a little bit of vegetable oil and then cook the breakfast sausages in this too. Put them aside in a dish, but don't add a paper towel to that dish. You want whatever oil drips from the bacon, here and there, for the calzone. Spread the dough into a rectangle either by hand or rolling pin with flour on the board or clean countertop. Layer the turkey ham, boiled ham, egg slices. Break sausages into small pieces, and add here and there. Finish with bacon. Drizzle whatever oil is in the dish that held the bacon and sausage all over. Roll up like a jelly roll. In a baking sheet, drizzle some olive oil in one line from top to bottom so you can roll the filled dough all around, ending with the open side at the bottom. Bake for 30 to 45 minutes, turning the baking sheet around after 25 minutes so it can brown on the other side evenly. Remove, cool, and slice as thin or as thick as you like.

I always have to make two or three of these because they eat them like there's no tomorrow!

DEVILED EGGS

6 hard-boiled eggs, each cut in half

Filling:
Egg yolks from the 6 hard boiled eggs, mash with fork and add: ¼ tsp salt
¼ tsp black pepper
½ tsp dry mustard
3 Tbsp salad dressing or vinegar, enough to moisten

Mix all together and fill the half egg-white shells.
Add bacon, sardines, or drizzled sausages for added taste.

WILD MUSHROOMS

If you or your hubby/friend are wild mushroom hunters, this recipe is for you.

Make sure that when you hunt for mushrooms, you look around and make sure that there are no metals (cans, nails, torn metals, etc) thrown into that area. Most mushrooms are good to eat, with very few exceptions, as long as you pick them from metal-free areas because metals are what makes mushrooms poisonous.

I like to clean my mushrooms individually by hand rather than put them in water and wash them. I cut a bit of the bottom of the stem off to see if it's clean with no deterioration. You are literally removing pine needles, sand, and leaves. Once you've cleaned them all, fill your sink halfway with warm water. Place them in a pail or a container large enough to hold them. In a very large boiling pot, fill it halfway with water. Place the cleaned mushrooms and 3 to 4 cloves of garlic, and close the lid. Each time it comes to boil, rinse the lid and clean the sides of the pan from all the dirt and whatever pine needles you've missed. Let it boil for 20 minutes. If the garlic doesn't turn black, they're safe to eat—they should be an off-white color. Drain in strainer and empty them into a pail that's been half filled with cold water. Drain them once a day for 3 days or until you don't see any more pine needles, dirt, etc. When you feel that they're clean enough to jar or freeze, squeeze as much water out of them as possible. Place them in the jar, filling the jar completely or filling the freezer bag completely; close it tightly. Don't overfill the jar, or the lid will not close completely, and they will turn bad. Just make sure you leave the top slightly unfilled before closing. Place the filled jars in the same pan you boiled the mushrooms in. Fill the pan with enough water to cover the jars. Place a clean kitchen cloth on top of the jars to cover them. Place a lid on the pan and boil for 30 minutes. If you freeze them, squeeze as much water out of them as possible, place in freezer bag and squeeze all the air out of the bag before closing. Place in another larger freezer bag to prevent freezer burns.

1 quart jar of preserved wild Mushrooms
1 clove of Garlic, diced
1 tsp Oregano
Salt and Pepper to taste
Red Pepper flakes to taste
2 tomatoes, crushed or diced, or 4 oz. of crushed tomatoes
½ cup of olive oil

Take the mushrooms out of the jar and place into a strainer. Rinse and squeeze the water out of them as much as possible. Place olive oil in frying pan on medium-high heat. Place mushrooms in pan. Sprinkle the diced garlic, oregano, red pepper flakes, salt, and pepper. Fry, stirring on and off, until they're almost dry to the look. Add about 3/4 cup of water, tomatoes, and a little salt on the tomatoes. Let them cook, stirring on and off, until the water has almost dried up and the mushrooms have plumped up. Taste for salt. Delicious as a side dish or a sandwich!

I have made this recipe with cutup celery, onions, peppers and whatever comes into my head at the time and it never fails me as to how delicious they are. I'll talk more about mushrooms in my next book – *Nonna's Kitchen 2.*

TRIPE

3 lbs of Tripe

Remove all fat (lard) from tripe. Cut tripe into 3-to 4-inch pieces, then boil in salted water with 1 squeezed lemon and remaining lemon rind or 1/3 cup white vinegar. Cut up and boil for 30 minutes or until tender. Pieces will shrink. You can do this a day or two ahead before cooking it.

Sauce:
1/3 cup of olive oil
1 clove of garlic, diced
1 small onion, diced
¼ tsp red pepper flakes (optional)
A little black pepper
¼ tsp each of mint, basil, oregano, parsley, and 2 bay leaves
8 to 10 oz. can crushed tomatoes
Salt to taste

In a saucepan, add oil, garlic, onion, and black pepper. Sauté until onion has wilted. Add the rest of the herbs and sauté for 1 more minute. Add a little of the crushed tomatoes, stir, and add the tripe. Cook/sauté for 2 minutes. Add the rest of the tomatoes and salt to taste. Add 1/3 cup of water, and cook until tender and the tomatoes have almost dried up. The sauce has to be on the tight side and not that wet. Taste for salt and hot pepper. Add more if you like.

LENTIL SOUP
1 large Soup Pot, filled almost 3/4 of the way with water
1 bag of Lentils, rinsed in water
1 stalk of Celery, washed and cut up in ¼ -inch thickness
1 Onion, diced
1 Clove of Garlic, diced
¼ cup of Olive Oil
1Tbsp Parsley
1 cup of Rice, boiled in 2 cups of water with salt and a drizzle of olive oil
Chicken meat pieces *(I usually use the rotisseried chicken leftover pieces or you can boil chicken thighs to use for this recipe—boiled in salted water until tender,*
Salt and Pepper to taste
Red Pepper flakes
Bay Leaf
Tiny Meatballs (optional)
2-3 Tbsp of chicken base

Rinse the lentils in water. Drain the water, and add the lentils to the water in the pot. Add salt (to taste, about 2 Tbsp or more) and olive oil. While it's cooking, it will foam. Remove this foam so the water stays clear. Cook for about 10 to 15 minutes until the lentils are al dente. Add the celery, onion, garlic, parsley, bay leaf, hot pepper flakes, chicken base and pepper. Cook until the celery is tender. Add the chicken pieces and/or meatballs and cook for 15 more minutes. Add the boiled rice. Taste for salt, take out Bay Leaf and serve with grated cheese. You can also make this soup without the chicken or meatballs. It's delicious either way.

Soup Meatballs:
1 cup fresh Italian bread crumbs
½ lb ground chuck meat (85 %) or sirloin
Salt and pepper to taste
1 tsp each of parsley and basil
1 small onion diced fine (optional)

1 small garlic clove diced fine (optional)
2-3 eggs
Sliver of olive oil
¼ cup of grated Romano cheese

Mix all together. Roll into small meatballs. Boil 1 in water to taste for salt. Add more salt if need be.   Add to soup or Lasagna/Casseroles.

HOLIDAY PUNCH
(Make ahead; non-alcoholic but it tastes like it is!)

You should make this punch ahead of time and leave it in closed liter bottles or jars until you're ready to use it. The older it is, the more it ferments and tastes like it has alcohol in it.

4 quarts of sugar-sweetened tea
½ can orange juice (not frozen)
1 to 2 cans grapefruit/orange juice
1 can pineapple juice
1 can crushed pineapple

Mix all together, and store in tightly closed litre bottles or jars or container until ready to use.

Great to make in September and use for the holidays!

When you're ready to make the punch, add ginger ale and sliced strawberries to taste and serve. Deliciously wonderful!

BEEF CUTLETS—Stuffed and Rolled
Eye Round Beef piece, partially frozen for easy cutting, and cut into thin slices that have been beaten with a knife.

Filling:
Fresh Italian breadcrumbs
Grated Romano cheese
Black pepper
Salt
Parsley
Garlic (optional)
Olive Oil, enough to just moisten the breadcrumbs

Mix all together. Fill each cutlet in the middle and roll. You can place a toothpick to keep each closed. Fry for 2 to 3 minutes in a pan with a little bit of olive oil. Or broil them on skewers for 2 to 3 minutes on each side.

BEEF TURNOVERS (Made at Christmastime)

Filling:
1 lb. ground beef—boiled in salted water
salt to taste
1 tsp parsley
2 beaten eggs
1 cup shredded mozzarella
½ cup grated parmesan cheese
¼ cup olive oil

Brown boiled beef in pan with oil, parsley, and salt for 2 minutes. Add beaten eggs and stir until cooked. Remove from heat. Add mozzarella and grated cheese. Taste for salt and cheese.

Dough:
2 cups of flour
A bit of olive oil
1 tsp salt
1/3 cup of warm water
1 egg

Mix all together, and knead until it has all come together and formed a nice soft dough. Keep adding flour and/or water to get that consistency. Cut pieces off dough and roll out into thin layers. Add a spoonful of filling. Cover the dough over the filling. Cut each turnover with a knife and close sides with a fork. Bake on an oil-greased baking sheet in a 375 to 400 degree oven or fry in olive oil on both sides.

SAUSAGES, PEPPERS AND ONIONS

1 lb. sweet and/or hot Italian pork sausages, boiled for 7 minutes, and
    then cut up:
4 Green Peppers, cored and cut in strips
2 Vidalia Onions, cut in strips
Mushrooms, cleaned and cut in half or quartered
¼ cup of Olive Oil
Salt to taste

In a frying pan, add a little olive oil and cut onions. Add salt to taste
and cook for 5 minutes, stirring on and off until almost starting to
wilt. Drain the onions into the dish that you will be placing this meal
into. Add a little more oil to the pan and add the sliced peppers. Add
salt to taste and cook for 5 minutes, stirring on and off until almost
starting to wilt. Drain the peppers into the dish with the onions. Add
more oil to the pan and fry mushrooms. Add salt to taste and cook
for 3 to 4 minutes. Take out with a slotted spoon and add to peppers
and onion dish. Add more oil to frying pan if needed and add the
sausages. Cook stirring on and off, until lightly browned on each side.
Add to vegetables and toss. Taste for salt and serve.

POTATOES AND EGGS

1 to 2 golden yellow potatoes, peeled and cut as thin french fries
5 eggs, beaten
salt and pepper to taste

Preheat a large (2 potatoes) or small frying pan (1 potato) on medium-high heat. Add sliced potatoes and cover, stirring on and off until potatoes are tender, testing with a fork.

To the beaten eggs, add salt and pepper and mix well. Add to fried potatoes all over, covering all the potatoes. Let it cook for a minute or so. It will bubble/rise up. Divide the potato mixture into fours, and turn each side over to cook the other side. Add some salt to the turned side. Turn them over again, and add some salt to that. By now, it should be completely cooked and lightly reddish colored. Place in a dish and serve by itself or in-between two pieces of bread as a sandwich.

This is my lifesaver when I have nothing to put out for a sandwich or lunch.

WALDORF SALAD

Lettuce Leaves
¾ cup diced Celery
1 cup peeled, cored, diced Apples
5 Tbsp chopped Walnuts
½ cup Mayonnaise

Wash and dry lettuce leaves. Line a salad bowl with the lettuce leaves. In a cereal bowl, mix the celery, apples, walnuts, and mayonnaise. Place mixture on the bed of leaves and serve.

GARDEN SALAD

½ Head of Iceberg Lettuce
Romaine Lettuce
Red Leaf Lettuce
½ Vidalia onion, washed and sliced nice and thin
Black Pitted Olives
Carrots, peeled and cut in thin 2-inch pieces
Nuts (optional)
Apples, Orange slices
Salt or Sea salt
Green and/or Red Peppers—sliced
Olive Oil or Vegetable Oil and vinegar (2 parts oil to 1 part vinegar) or 1
    lemon, squeezed
1 Cucumber—peeled, sliced or cut in half widthwise, then cut in
    half lengthwise again and then cut into 1-2 inch pieces (crunchy!)

Cut and wash the salads by hand to whatever size you want. Drain.
Place in salad bowl. Add onions, olives, nuts, fruits, cucumbers,
peppers and carrots. Add salt. Add oil and vinegar or 1 squeezed
lemon juice. Toss, taste for salt and serve.

POTATO AND STRING BEAN SALAD (Italian Style)

4 Yukon Gold or yellow potatoes
1 lb. of String Beans, snipped, snapped in half, and washed
Sea Salt
¼ cup of Extra Virgin Olive oil
3 Tbsp of Wine Vinegar (or more, if you like to taste a lot of vinegar)
1 Garlic, finely diced
½ tsp of crushed Oregano

Boil the potatoes in water, covering all the potatoes in a covered pan. Cook for 30 minutes covered from the time you put the heat on. After 20 minutes, add the string beans and cover for the rest of the remaining time. Drain. Let it cool a little so the potatoes are easy to handle when you have to peel the skin off.

After peeling the skin off the potatoes, place in a salad bowl or dish large enough to hold the potatoes and string beans, cut them in half, then in half the other way, and then cut the whole potato in halves or thirds depending on the size you want. Add the string beans on top of the potatoes, then the diced garlic, oregano, sea salt, oil, and vinegar. Toss and taste for salt, adding more salt if needed. Serve.

PRESERVING

LUPINI BEANS

Buy a bag of dry lupini beans or as much as you want to preserve.

Soak the lupini beans in water for three days. Then boil them until the skin turns white (boil about 1½ to 2 hours). Rinse and drain them.

Place them in fresh water for another three days, changing the water morning and night.

Add salt on the second and third days. Put them in jars, adding a little salt to the top of the filled jar. Close the jar and refrigerate. Before eating them, taste for salt. If they're a bit salty, replace the water with fresh cold water without salt. That will take a lot of the salt out. If it's still too salty, repeat the freshwater process.

EGGPLANTS

There are two different ways to preserve eggplants. Both are equally delicious eaten by themselves or in a sandwich with deli meats:

1. Peel the eggplants. Cut them, shoestring style. Layer them on a board, adding salt to each layer, and finish by placing a heavy object on top so it squeezes the juice out of them for 24 hours. Place them in a bowl. Add oregano, hot red pepper flakes, and enough olive oil to saturate them. Taste for salt. Place them in a jar and cover tightly until you're ready to use them.

2. Peel the eggplants. Cut them wide shoestring style. Place them on brown paper bags, or string them with needle and thread, and hang them up to dry, preferably in a sunny area. When they've dried, boil them in a pan filled with 2 cups of water and 1 cup of white distilled vinegar until they revive their natural body. Place in a bowl. Add salt, oregano, red pepper flakes, diced garlic, and olive oil. Place in jar, and pour enough olive oil to cover the top of the eggplants. Close tightly and keep in a cool place.

GREEN TOMATO PICKLES

1 Peck or 8 Quarts of Green Tomatoes, sliced
12 onions
1½ oz black pepper
1 oz whole allspice
¼ lb ground mustard
1 oz whole cloves
1 oz mustard seeds
½ cup coarse salt
Vinegar

Arrange tomatoes and onions in layers, sprinkling salt between layers. Let stand overnight. Drain. Add remaining ingredients. Cover with vinegar and simmer gently for 15 minutes. Pack into clean hot jars. Seal at once.

JARRING FRESH TOMATOES

Make sure tomatoes are nice and ripe and red. A lot of fresh basil, rinsed with clear cold water.

Purchase quart or pint Mason jars or a combination of both. Rinse them through the dishwasher or by hand.

Wash the tomatoes thoroughly. If they're small, leave whole, otherwise cut into halves or quarters and place them in a large bowl big enough to hold a lot of tomatoes. When you've filled the bowl with the cut tomatoes, salt them a little and mix them so the salt kisses all of the tomatoes.

In each jar, place 2 or 3 basil leaves at the bottom. Fill each jar with the whole or cut tomatoes, pressing them down with a wooden spoon so there's no air between the tomato pieces. Fill each jar to a half inch at the top. Add 2 basil leaves and cover the jar tightly. Place jars in a 5 quart or more boiling pan. Add enough warm water to cover the top of the jars. Place a clean kitchen cloth over all the jars in the pan. Cover and boil for 20 to 25 minutes. Remove with a tong and place on board or counter. Check the lids to make sure that each jar is securely closed or else the tomatoes will go bad on you. Keep them in a cool place. One thing I've learned is that some tomatoes are acidy, and you can tell by looking at the bottom of the tomato jar when you're ready to use them. If you see a whitish soot, I would throw the tomatoes away unless you're willing to add A LOT of sugar to take that acid away. If you just see the basil leaves and tomatoes on the bottom that are nice and clear, they'll be delicious for your needs.

NOTE: *Garden tomatoes sometimes tend to have or be more acidy then farm bought tomatoes or tomatoes purchased by the bushel at your local produce or fruit store.*

JARRING FRESH STRING BEANS

Wash them thoroughly. Cut them or leave whole. Boil in salted water for 3 minutes. Pack them in Mason jars while hot, and finish filling the jars with the hot water about ¼ to ½ inch from the top of the jars. Boil jars, adding enough water to cover the top of the jars, and keep covered with a cloth on top of all the jars in the pan for about 30 to 45 minutes. Cool the jars for 24 hours and keep them in a cool spot after that.

FREEZING BEANS

If you wish to freeze the beans, boil them in salted water for 3 minutes, cool, and pack in a plastic freezer bag, pressing the air out of the bag. Place into another freezer bag and freeze.

CRANBERRY RELISH, FRESH

This is a very easy and delicious cranberry relish that goes wonderfully both with your Thanksgiving turkey and with the sandwiches you make from the leftovers. It takes barely five minutes to prepare.

2 12 oz. bags fresh cranberries
1 large navel orange (or 2 small ones; modify to your liking)
¼ to 1/3 cup sugar or to taste
2 Tbsp cognac or Grand Marnier
¼ to ½ cup slivered almonds

Freeze cranberries for at least an hour (but up to a year). Rinse briefly, pick over, and toss into food processor. Cut orange into quarters, then cut each quarter crosswise in half. Do not peel. Add orange sections to food processor. Add sugar and liqueur of choice. Process in very brief pulses until ingredients are finely chopped but not mushy. Taste and adjust amount of sugar if desired. Turn out into serving bowl and gently stir in almonds. Serve chilled.

Printed in Great Britain
by Amazon